THE INDIAN FISCAL PROBLEM

THE INDIAN FISCAL PROBLEM

BEING A COURSE OF SEVEN LECTURES DELIVERED AT PATNA UNIVERSITY IN AUGUST 1923

J.C. COYAJEE

GYAN

Published by

Gyan Publishing House
5, Ansari Road
Daryaganj, New Delhi-110002
Phone: 011-47034999, 9811692060
E-mail: books@gyanbooks.com

Distribution Network
gyanbooks.com
India, USA, Canada, UK, Australia

ISBN: 978-93-7225-236-1 (PB)

First Published, 1923

2nd Impression 2025

Printed at: Gyan Press, Delhi.

THE INDIAN FISCAL PROBLEM
Author: J.C. COYAJEE

THE INDIAN FISCAL PROBLEM

BEING

A COURSE OF SEVEN LECTURES

DELIVERED AT PATNA UNIVERSITY

IN

AUGUST, 1923.

BY

J. C. COYAJEE,

Member, Indian Fiscal Commission,

Professor of Economics in Presidency College, Calcutta.

ESSE QUAM VIDERI MALIM

CALCUTTA:

PRINTED AT THE ART PRESS AND PUBLISHED BY

PATNA UNIVERSITY, PATNA.

—

1924.

PREFACE.

The University of Patna did me the honour in 1923 to appoint me Banaili Reader in Indian Economics, and I was asked to deliver a course of lectures during the session 1923-1924. The theoretical position taken up, and the policy recommended in these lectures are practically identical with those of the Majority report of the Indian Fiscal Commission, though I have availed myself of the present opportunity to develop further the theoretical considerations underlying fiscal policy, and to draw attention to the lessons and warnings in which the tariff history of the last century is so rich. Anything like an exhaustive treatment of the numerous important aspects of tariff policy, history and administration was, of course, not possible within the range of a few lectures; but I hope to be able to follow up the present publication by a more comprehensive study of tariff-making in theory and practice.

Perhaps the one merit that I might claim for these lectures is the absence of a partisan spirit. While I believe in the ultimate success of a policy of discriminating protection judiciously carried out, I have not striven to disguise the fact that the nation must be prepared to make the necessary sacrifice in various directions. Again, at a time when India is making up its mind on the subject of its tariff policy, it seems to me desirable to place clearly before the public the views and pronouncements of the great masters of fiscal theory and history, irrespective of the school to which they happen to belong.

I wish to express my cordial thanks to Mr. Prafulla Kumar Sarkar, M.A., who has assisted me at every stage of the preparation of this book—from its inception in my Economics Seminar to its passing through the press.

CALCUTTA, J. C. C.
February, 1924.

CONTENTS.

LECTURE I.

ARGUMENTS FOR PROTECTION.

The Indian Fiscal Commission, which was appointed to examine the tariff policy of the Government of India, has come to the conclusion that in the interest of the country, the policy of discriminating protection should be adopted. The task of carrying out such investigations affecting the whole range of the fiscal policy of a great country is one of the most difficult in the field of applied Economics. The sifting and appraising of the arguments for either system of fiscal policy is, in itself, no easy affair. Centuries of controversy have strewn the ground with weapons, good, bad and indifferent, and the reasons for a judicious and discriminating policy have to be separated from mere appeals to popular prejudice. The theoretical difficulties in the way of the Commission were not inconsiderable—to analyse the assumptions on which free-trade theory is based, to estimate how far the assumptions were justificable or not, and on the basis of this analysis to found the case for any advisable departures in the protectionist direction. Again, in studying the possible effects of a protectionist policy a proper perspective has to be maintained, and great care has to be exercised to distinguish between the immediate and long-period effects of protectionist measures. The confusion between these two sets of effects has been the source of much fallacious reasoning, as we shall notice later on. On the practical side, the difficulties of anticipating the effects of any proposed fiscal system are still greater. It is a complicated problem to examine the full case for protection as regards any single industry—to balance the sacrifice to be made and the burden to be borne both by consumers and by other industries, against the potentialities of gain to the industry in question. But the complexity of the problem is vastly increased when the possibilities of simultaneous protection to a number of industries are being contemplated. The items of loss and gain are then so numerous and complicated that it is difficult to guess and impossible to compute the resultant balance ; and yet any judgment as to a protectionist policy would be hopelessly faulty which tried to envisage its potentialities as regards individual industries, and did not try to make some estimate of the consequences both to the consumers and to the entire industrial system.

Rationale of free trade.

The rationale of free-trade admits of brief and clear exposition. It has been asserted, that as in every particular exchange there is necessarily a gain to each of the parties concerned, "the sum total of such exchanges should be allowed to attain the maximum volume so as to yield a maximum satisfaction to consumers." *Prima facie,* international trade brings a gain and any restriction on it presumably a loss. From these axioms is deduced the practical rule of free trade that all efforts to direct the productive forces of the country in any particular direction artificially should be given up. "The most effective way of promoting progress would seem to be to make the way, free and open for the best producer wherever he be."

Rationale of protection.

The correct theory of protection is based upon the unfulfilled assumptions and necessary qualifications of the naive free-trade theory. As a great master has pointed out we cannot use as convertible, the two phrases "the commodities which a country can now produce most easily", and "the commodities which a country has the greatest potential advantages for producing". There might be reasons for looking much beyond the present interests of the consumer and the present capacities of the local producer. The benefits of international division of labour are no doubt great ; but it is only when fully developed countries compete as equals that the best form of international division of labour can be reached, and such a division is itself reached only by tentative stages. In the popular statements of free-trade theory it is further assumed that "so long as the capital and other resources of a country can be employed with equal profit the method of application is a matter of indifference." Finally, the transfer of capital and labour from one industry to another, as the result of the stress of foreign competition, is a much more formidable matter than has sometimes been supposed. The unfulfilled assumptions and the unemphasised qualifications of free-trade form the armoury of protection. In the considerations stated above might be recognised the leading arguments for protection.

The Young Industries argument.

In advancing and marshalling the arguments for protection the Indian Fiscal Commission has justly given the place of honour to the infant industries argument. Not only is the theoretical validity of the agrument undeniable but there has been a tendency to extend the scope of its application on the part of recognised economic authorities. By parity of reasoning, the extension of protection has been recommended even to older industries which are suffering from temporary atrophy—such industries being regarded as infants *pro tempore*. The Commission has duly noted this; but there is also another proposed line of extension of the argument. As Prof. Taussig has argued, there is scope for protection to young industries even in the case of old countries which have fairly entered upon the manufacturing stage. Obviously, however, this line of reasoning should not be carried too far. The assistance to be given to infant industries must vary with the difficulties in their way ; and the general industrial development of a country cannot but diminish in a great measure the initial difficulties of industries started later. With the general industrial development a class of efficient entrepreneurs must have been trained up, capital must have been accumulated and a skilled labour force brought into existence ; hence, Prof. Taussig himself qualifies his remarks by adding that the opportunity for the use of protection in the case of industrially advanced countries is to be limited to "periods of transition and of great industrial change."

Its increasing scope and importance.

What should be emphasized here is, that not only the scope of the argument but the weight and importance of the considerations lying behind it have been constantly increasing with the growth of the complexity and scale of business enterprise. The advantage always enjoyed by established enterprise has been greatly increased by the growth of massive production, the massive treatment of by-products and by the internal and external economies corresponding to the expansion of business units and industries. Capital is needed on an ever increasing scale to compete with large manufacturing establishments abroad. The natural advantages of large scale production are multiplied by the powers developed through integrations and combinations. On the othed hand, the natural protection enjoyed by domestic industries is being constantly diminished by improvements in transportation and the reduction of freights. All these factors add to the difficulties of starting new industries in a country. But even this is not the full measure of the difficulties under which infant industries labour in our days. Neither Mill nor List knew of the present day policies of cutting out foreign rivals—export bounties open or concealed, special transportation rates for export business, and specially reduced prices of commodities sold or export. Had those writers been living to-day, they would have been even more convinced advocates of the theory of protection to young industries. Who, for example, can doubt that if India had delayed the initiation of her cotton industry by half a century, and were starting it in these days, that nascent industry would soon have been dumped out of existence?

Then again, the case for protection to nascent industries has been to a certain extent strengthened in another direction by the growth of massive production. On this subject some dicta of Dr. Marshall might be carefully studied as showing the exact limits within which the advocate of protection to infant industries can take advantage of this circumstance as favouring his contention. "It is obvious that an industry which offers large scope for the economies of massive production stands to gain much from protective duties, if they can be so arranged as to insure it the almost undisturbed possession of the home market while keeping open for it opportunities for large sales abroad: its sales at home and its sales abroad, alike increase its command over economies that help it to undersell rivals in neutral markets." In another place he observes that "it may be admitted that there is some force in the claim that a protective tariff is needed to aid giant businesses in establishing a complete standardization on the most advanced modern model." While thus the argument for protection to nascent industries is strengthened, to a certain extent, it does not follow that we should benefit by extending protection to all national industries conforming to increasing returns. In the first place, we must have regard to the circumstance that "many of the advantages which a single industry derives from a protective duty in its favour, involves loss and hindrance to other industries." Nor can we afford to forget that economies of massive production are of many different kinds, and that while protection might influence some of these economies it might adversely affect the others. Nevertheless after making allowance for these considerations, we might recognize the existence of beneficial potentialities in the extension of protection to wisely chosen manufactures which have "great latent powers of economy through production on a large scale". Finally, it cannot be denied that the more any country exports "her raw produce in return for manufactures the less benefit she will get from the Law of Increasing Return". The application of the last remark to conditions obtaining in India is obvious.

---

*On this topic the student should refer to Marshall, *Industry and Trade*, pp. 138, 746 & 764; also to the same author's *Money Credit and Commerce*, p. 218.

We might now turn our attention to the other cogent argument on behalf of protection—that for the diversification of industries—which, during the last century or so has been formulated in many different ways and presented from many angles of vision. Alexander Hamilton had noted how diversification of industry helped to afford a more ample and various field for enterprise and to furnish greater scope for the diversity of talents and dispositions. List had argued from a different point of view for "the principle of the variety and division of occupations and the co-operation of the national productive powers." He pointed out the importance of such co-ordination and diversification as regards the social condition of a nation, and showed that the general well-being of a people depended upon the balance and harmony of their producive powers. The illustration by which List enforces his proposition seems to be particularly applicable to Indian conditions. "It is", he says "possible for a nation to possess too many philosophers, philologers, and literati and too few skilled artisans, merchants, and seamen. This is the consequence of highly advanced and learned culture which is not supported by advanced manufacturing power." Coming to more recent times, we find that in the latter part of the nineteenth century the same argument was brought into great prominence owing to what appeared to be the excessive and one-sided industrial development of Germany. This led economists like Wagner to emphasize—and even to over-emphasize—the importance of an all-round development of a nation in industrial matters. Any other policy would be followed, says Wagner "at the cost of a one-sided occupation of its population, the narrowing of their views, the most one-sided physical and mental development, the absence of all the advantages of the universality and variety of national production, and of the favourable reaction of this upon the national life in general". He professes to look at this question not exclusively as a problem

Formulation of the argument for diversified industry.

of economic value but from the point of view of "the abiding interest of the nation's economy, of its civilization, of the national life as a whole". Though the views of Wagner have been denounced as pessimistic by Schmoller, who held more moderate opinions of the subject, yet Schmoller himself was in favour of employing moderate duties so as to develop both the agrarian and the industrial strength of his country.

It might have been noted that the two arguments—the infant industry argument and the argument relating to diversification and correlation of industries—are closely related, the one referring to the development and the other to the co-ordination and co-operation of productive powers. The development of any particular infant industry is one means and aspect of securing the requisite national co-ordination of industries. But in looking at diversification or co-ordination of industries, our view points is shifted to the national outlook embracing all industries and to their inter-relations. Our outlook is in fact widened and we look not only to the interactions of industries and their equilibrim but to the reaction of the whole scheme of industries on the national psychology and temperament. This wide range of the diversified industry argument imports into it considerations relating to all aspects of protection—social, psychological, and industrial. But it also makes that wide topic the breeding ground of dangerous fallacies like the home market argument, indiscriminate protection and "autarchy".

Like the infant industry argument the argument for diversity of industry loses much of its force in the case of the more advanced manufacturing countries. Thus, a great authority on matters of fiscal policy expresses the view that "in view of the degree of industrial activity which is certain to appear under any circumstances in a modern country of advanced civilization, this sort of vague allegation has no probative force." But, in the case of a country like India it is far otherwise; and the best argument for diversification of industries is furnished by the statistics of industrial employees in India which are most instructive and which show either the non-existence or the insignificant beginnings of numerous industries of the first order of national importance. These statistics bring to our mind and give a fresh significance to Dr. Marshall's dictum: "A new country may be dominantly rural, may lack the stimulus and culture of a nervous town-life, and have no access to the economies of manufacture on a large scale: she will then derive comparatively little consolation from knowing that there are busy hives of industry and thought in remote lands." Nor need we be afraid of applying this dictum about "new countries" to India since the same writer has remarked on the possibilities of rejuvenation of older countries provided they listen to the gospel of self-sacrifice and of industrialisation.

It has often been asserted that the basis and ground-work of Indian protectionism is the infant industry argument. That, however, is not the case. While the argument from diversity of industry has been receding in importance in the advanced Western countries it has always been to the fore in India. It required some theoretical preparation to understand the infant industry argument; but no one could fail to remark the lack of diversity of industry in this country. In fact, Ranade who opened the fiscal controversy in India, dwelt most on the "ruralisation" or "rustication" of India—these being only strong expressions for the lack of diversified industry. The Famine Commissioners in their Report of 1880 had argued that no remedy for the evils of famines could be complete which did not include the introduction of a diversity of occupations, through which the surplus population might be drawn from agricultural pursuits and be led to find the means of subsistence in manufactures. Ranade followed this up with the view that "a due co-ordination of the three-fold forms of industrial activity, even if it be not immediately, most advantageous to individuals in any one period, is a permanent national insurance against recurrent dangers, and, as such is economically the most beneficent course in the interests of the community". He further emphasised the unfortunate effects of the lack of diversity of industry on the social and intellectual side—as transferring the monopoly not only of wealth, but what is more important, of skill, talent and activity to others. His disciple, Mr. G. V. Joshi, "regarded the dependence of the people on agriculture as the sole means of subsistence as the weakest point in India's economic position and pleaded for the co-ordination of agricultural and manufacturing industries with the direct help of the state." This train of reasoning was reinforced by historical reminiscences of the days when India possessed a series of relatively strong domestic industries and emphasis was laid on this aspet of the matter by the late Mr. Romesh Chunder Dutt and Pandit Malaviya among others. In his evidence before the Fiscal Commission, Prof. Jevons advanced and ably summarised this traditional case for India in the matter of diversification of industries. He gave a new turn to the old "ruralisation" argument by pointing to the fact that, excepting the great ports and one or two inland industrial towns, there are no great industrial centres in India, and that the towns of Northern India have been for years in a state of industrial decay. This is a pointed restatement of Ranade's complaint as to the "rustication" of India. What is wanted urgently is a period of industrial reconstruction in India which might stimulte the growth of new inland towns and the revival of some of the old cities. The social and educational advantages of diversified industry were also brought out clearly: "The buzz and huzz of industries, the increased profits and earnings of the people, the changed mental outlook which is stimulated by progress and success in one's immediate locality, would have an almost unimaginable influence upon the national temperament and character. When industries become established and thriving occupations of various kinds become open to all men, and every man can take up that which suits him best, a ladder of advancement is opened and with it the buoyancy of hope, which stimulates to work and enterprise."

It has recently been argued that the extent to which an

opportunity for the employment of educated Indians would be afforded by the development of industries is often exaggerated. We can well understand that the posts of an important directive character which can be made available as the result of industrial development would not be as many as are sometimes supposed. But the mere number of the posts of directive importance is no accurate measure of the influence exerted by the industrial stimulus in affording practical training of a business character to the youth of India. The leavening influence exerted by the opening up of such employments is of many times greater value than the jobs themselves; nor can it be said with truth that it is only the employment of a directive character which will have such influence, since so far as the skilled artisan class or the class of well-paid foremen increases the practical instincts and abilities will be materially strengthened. If we compute the aggregate both of those engaged in the work of direction and of those who are doing supervising and skilled mechanical work, the potential increase of talents of a practical character appears to be of a substantial character.

While desiring to secure the diversification of national industries by all judicious means, we must not let ourselves forget that such industrialisation has got some social drawbacks and possesses a less favourable side. The Fiscal Commission was fully aware that industrial development will bring in new and pressing problems—many of them arising from the aggregation of population in large towns. Again, poverty and unemployment might assume forms hitherto unknown in India and might demand new machinery to cope with them. These do form deductions from the beneficial consequences of industrial development, but they form no argument against undertaking such development. Much could be done to avoid these evils by the utilization of resources available to us in the shape of proper town-planning, housing, general sanitation and wise factory legislation. A wise guide in the field of economics would have us take a balanced view of the matter. It is true, he would say, that industrial development leads not only to urban aggregation of multitudes, but to a constantly increasing inequality of wealth due to concentration of ownership and management in the field of manufacturing enterprise. But, on the other hand, he would remind us that, socially speaking, the operatives in the manufacturing districts of industrially developed countries are generally far from being worse off than the agricultural workers of industrially undeveloped countries. Finally, he would have us note that "after all, the mode in which an industry is conducted, and the character of the people engaged in it are far more important than the nature of the industry itself."

Nevertheless it is peculiarly easy to exaggerate the scope of the argument for diversification of industries and we would do well to bear in mind the *limitations of the argument.* It is too often assumed that the domestic production of an article is in itself a national benefit apart from the natural advantages which a country might possess in the matter of its production. In fact, the principle of comparative costs is in some danger of being forgotten in the jubilation resultant upon what is considered to be the acquisition of a new industry for the country. The truth is that the aquisition of industries for which a country has no comparative advantage is a diversion of labour and capital from more profitable employment and hence a waste of national resources. The principle of comparative cost defines the scope of wise diversification of industry. "The real question", as Taussig observes, "is which of the two ways of securing the goods in question is the better. To make a thing at home is not to our advantage if we make it at a high cost. To import it is not a source of loss when we import a thing more cheaply than we make it at home. Let us hold fast to the fundamental principle that exports are the means of producing the imports, and that only if there be real effectiveness, real success in the application of our labour and capital, does the country gain." The greater the size of a country the stronger is the case for diversification, but the temptation to apply protection beyond the judicious limits also increases. An extensive geographical area invites a diversification of industry, since it is likely that the variety of raw materials required for any industry would be found scattered somewhere over the region. But, if these materials are located by nature very far apart from each other, the cost of assembling them might add largely to the other costs of the industry and hamper it permanently, and sometimes to too great an extent, in its competition with foreign rivals. A wise location of the industry becomes in such conditions a highly complicated problem, and sometimes the great distances involved might make the solution impossible.

It would be easy to quote warnings, even from leading economists of the protectionist school, against using protection too far in the interests of diversification of national industry. There is an obvious limit to the utilization of protection with this object. Protectionist authorities like Schüller recognize that even an advanced industrial state should not attempt to produce all the objects required for its growing consumption and that it should be always content to import numerous articles. They admit that as result of a misuse of industrial protection the gain from the increased production is much smaller than the combined loss caused on the one hand to the consumer and on the other to the export trade.

Some protectionist writers have asserted like Patten that protection is necessary to keep society in a dynamic state. So far as this assertion has any significance it must be the application of protection to young industries which alone can have the effect desired. As industrial development progresses, new industries come into existence as well as new branches or grades of old industries. Protection to these can be always given advisedly and under proper circumstances, and it is in this sense only that protection is required to keep industrial society dynamic. On the other hand, protection given indirectly to old industries or to all industries without regard to the principle of comparative advantage in production, results in industrial stagnation or in a static condition in the sense understood by Patten.

The revenue argument for protection does not appear to be a strong one and was in fact over-emphasized by the Fiscal Commission. There are two propositions which appear to be very similar but are really quite different. The first of these propositions is that a high revenue tariff incidentally affords some protection to manufactures ; the other is that a high revenue can be derived from a protectionist tariff. The determining factor of the revenue-yielding capacity of a duty is the elasticity of the demand for the dutiable article. So far as protectionist considerations raise a duty above the point of maximum productivity, the result is a diminution of revenue. So far, again, as the tariff reduces the real income of the consuming classes the total revenue must be reduced. Great care has to be taken, when dealing with the revenue aspect of protection to *keep apart the short-period and the long period effects.* It is quite possible that in the long period a successful application of protection will raise the total of the revenue-yielding capacity of the country ; but no such result can be looked for within several decades ; the more so that the infancy stage of industries tends to grow longer with the growing complexity and scale of industries.

Effect of protection on the aggregate revenues.

Those persons who believe that protection will merely transfer in the near future the field of revenue earnings from the imported goods to the wealth created in the country, are to be envied for their optimism but not for their knowledge of tariff history. They are, in fact, mixing up the short-period and long-period effects of the introduction of protection. It is true that if protection succeeds in bringing on a marked industrial development, the tax-paying capacity of the country will increase the yield from income-tax, customs, etc. But that consummation is a matter of many decades, as the experience even of great and go-ahead countries like the United States of America shows. Thus, Taussig tells us that in spite of the unsurpassed mechanical skill and natural resources of that country, the iron industry had to be protected as an infant industry for about thirty years. As the same author has shown, during the above period (1875 to 1897) protection must have enabled the American iron-masters to make profits at the expense of the consumers, and no doubt they paid over a small portion of these profits to their Government in the shape of taxes; but these profits for the three decades could not be said to have *added* to the tax-bearing capacity of the country as a whole. All such profits were made at the expense of the American purchasers of iron and steel; and, as these purchasers thus paid a heavy tax to the local producers in the shape of higher prices, the capacity of the former to pay taxes to their Government must be taken to have been correspondingly reduced. It is obvious, in short, that during the period of infancy of industries there is no possibility of any increase of the aggregate tax-paying capacity of the country; there can be only a redistribution of resources within the country—the consumers losing what the protected producers gain. It is only after the infant industries have reached the stage of maturity that the aggregate national dividend and wealth can be said to have increased; and then alone can it be asserted that the taxable wealth of the nation has grown. Here, and as we shall see later in the whole study of the influence of protection on trade and finance, we have to be careful in distinguishing between immediate and long-period results. Taussig once believed that the period of infancy of an industry under the fostering care of protection was a decade or thereabouts. But he goes on to say: "An opinion of this sort I should not now support. What has already been said of the tenacity of old habits, and the difficulties of new enterprises justifies the contention that a generation more, or less, may elapse before it is clear whether success has been really attained." And, if new industries take as much three decades to grow to adolescence in that land of push and hustle, they will surely require a longer time in our country where "we are conervative to a fault", and where not only powers of industrial organization but the necessary basic as well as subsidiary industries have yet to be created. Something also must be allowed for the constantly growing scale and complexity of industry in general which must necessarily tend to prolong the stage of infancy.

Effect of protection on the customs revenue.

If we regard the yield of protectionist import duties by themselves, the revenue-yielding capacity of protectionist finance would appear to be greatly over-rated. The case of Japan has been expressly referred to in the minority note as showing that protective duties are "a reservoir of national wealth." But it cannot be said to be a very happy illustration. We can go into the comparison between Indian and Japanese customs revenues in two ways. In the first place, we might consider what proportion of the total national revenue is formed by the customs revenue in the case of each country. Taking the year 1920-21, we find that in India, the customs revenue formed over 21 per cent. of the total revenue, that it contributed the largest item of revenue, that its yield was above 50 per cent, larger than that of the income-tax, and was nearly thrice the yield from stamps. In the case of Japan the customs revenue formed 74 million yens out of a total revenue of 1,562 million yens or out of an ordinary revenue of 1,237 millions yens, *i.e.*, about 6 per cent. The customs duties yielded in Japan about one fourth of what the income-tax produced (268 millions yens), and the customs revenue was smaller than the yield from the excise on sugar and textile fabrics. The excise duty on textile fabrics brought in about half the amount of the customs revenue. Again, the customs revenue of Japan was much less than half of what was yielded by the Japanese post, telegraph and telephone services (187 millions yens).

The other way of looking at the matter is to examine the elasticity of the customs revenue in each country and to see how it compares with the rate at which other items of the national revenues have grown. In India,

	1904-05. Rs.	1921-22. Rs.
Customs	6½ crores.	34½ crores.
Excise	8 ,,	17 ,,
Stamps	5½ ,,	11 ,,
Income-tax	2 ,,	22 ,,

In the case of Japan,*

	1904-05.			1921-22.		
Customs	23	millions	Yens.	74	millions	Yens.
Excise	14½	,,	,,	75	,,	,,
Stamps	17	,,	,,	69	,,	,,
Income-tax	14½	,,	,,	268	,,	,,

The base year 1904-1905 has been chosen, because about that time Japan entered upon the paths of protection. The rate of increase of customs revenue in Japan is much smaller than the increase of other items of revenue and is also smaller than the rate of growth of the customs revenue of India.

In the case of Germany, although the yield from import duties is large on the whole, the revenue from the duties on manufactured goods was small. Ashley computed that only about one-fifth of the German customs revenue was obtained from duties on manufactured goods while the duties on food, drink, tobacco and cereals produced nearly one half. The protectionist character of a duty does not in any way improve its capacity and value as an instrument of finance; that capacity depends mainly on the elasticity of demand for the dutiable article on the part of the country levying the duty. Nor is this principle unknown to the high protectionists of Germany. For in 1902 when the duties were raised on both agricultural and manufactured imports no pretence was made of obtaining any additional income from the latter source. The figures for 1913 showed that in the case of Germany the protective duties on foodstuffs contributed 41.2 per cent. of the total customs

*Cf. the fifteenth Financial and Economic Annual of Japan pp. 14-15; also The Japan Year Book, 1921-22, pp. 400, and 502.

revenue, while the protective duties on manufactures, high though they were, supplied only 15.5 per cent. of the net revenue. So also in the case of the United States of America, as regards the yield of revenue the leading items consist of duties on sugar, molasses and tobacco. These three articles contributed about half the customs revenue. Taking the ten leading items contributing about 79 per cent. of the revenue we come to find out that duties on manufactures yield about a fourth of the total. France obtains an even smaller proportion of her revenue from duties on manufactured articles the leading items in the order of relative importance being—coffee, cereals, mineral oils, machine and tools, and cocoa.*

The wages argument.

The wages argument for protection has been also perhaps over-emphasised by the Indian Fiscal Commission. As high authorities put it, the direct influence of protection on wages has been exaggerated. Schmoller goes so far as to say that the wages argument for protection is one of the weakest. He urges in support of this view that there are other influences acting upon wages which are of far greater importance than fiscal policy. He advises "the intelligent labouring class of Germany and its enlightened leaders" to accept protection rather in the general interest of industrial development than in the particular interest of their class. He quotes and agrees with Sir Charles Dilke whose view was that in Canada and Australia protection had neither raised nor lowered general wages.† Professor Taussig's opinion on this subject is the same. According to him "No respectable writer or teacher would say for a moment that high wages are due to the tariff or that the maintenance of a high range of general wages (observe, we speak of general wages) is dependent on the tariff. The main cause of generous wages is at bottom a very simple one: generous productiveness of industry.‡

*Gregory *Tariffs*, pp. 497-498.
†Schmoller, *op. cit;* Vol. II, p. 644.
‡Taussig, *Free Trade, the Tariff and Reciprocity*, p. 141.

This makes possible the combination of money wages that are higher than in other countries with prices that are as low as in other countries or lower."

The above views of the economists depend upon the fact that in the long run, the source of higher wages is higher efficiency of labour, and if high wages are secured by any form of fiscal policy for inefficient labour that can be only at the cost of the consumer. Again, high nominal wages might be secured by the action of fiscal policy to labour, but that does not mean that the real wages are high, since wage-earners will lose as consumers what they gain as producers. Still, one can understand to a certain extent the emphasis laid by some advocates of protection on the wages argument. Because, although an efficient labour force is a condition precedent of sound industrial development, yet on the other hand, industrial development also reacts on the efficiency of labour by placing before it a greater scope for its productive powers and by introducing it to more efficient methods of work carried on with the co-operation of superior machinery. Thus, in the long period, there is some interaction between industrial development on sound lines and the wages of labour. It might also be added that protection can be conceivably so directed and carried out as to cause a substantial increase of real wages, although in practice no country has adopted that form of protection. The labouring class will be favoured directly by a tariff, if it was employed to build up by artificial means those industries in which labour is the principal factor. Such a policy might injure other industries and yet benefit labour on the whole. However, the ingenious devisor of this idea, Professor Carver, admits that as protection has been actually carried out in different countries, its object has been to assist the capitalist class, because the influence of capitalism on politics is much greater than that of labour. Nor is there any prospect that protection will be used in any country to advance the interest of labour at the expense of those of capital.

In India much has been made of the argument that protection will develop the resources of our capitalists and industrialists by increasing the dividends going to them. In other countries the advocates of protection prefer to be reticent as regards this tendency; for, while in one aspect the existence of such a possibility is an argument in favour of protection, in another aspect it is a great admission. The implication is that protection adds to the strength, spirit and resource of capitalism, and that it enables capital to take toll from the consuming class; though, of course, the capitalist would add that he could invest the resources thus transferred to him in a better way. Indeed we are now at the stage where, as some writers put it, the argument for protection to infant industries is extended into an argument for protection to infant capitalism or finance. No one can deny the interdependence between the development of industry and that of finance; at the same time, it is also certain that the increase of capital so far as it is fostered by protection is to a considerable extent at the expense of the domestic consumer. Manufacturing development on protectionist lines admittedly intensifies the inequalities of distribution. As a recent writer on the protectionist side puts it "effective protection to manufactures would act as a force striking the plain of wealth—distribution, and crumpling it up into hills and valleys". There can be no sort of doubt that protection tends to concentrate wealth at the cost of the consuming public; the saving feature is that "it will concentrate it in the hands of people who are well-nigh inevitable savers."

Protection and national capital resources.

But there is another aspect of the argument, so far as India is concerned, which deserves to be noted here. It seems fairly obvious, that if a protectionist policy can draw out money from the hoards into productive circulation it might render a real service. It so happens, however, that one of the leading economists of India has expressed his disagreement with this view. According to him the money drawn from the hoards will only cause a temporary rise of prices and a resultant increase of imports, and then such money will leave the country. In answer to this chain of reasoning it is submitted here, that in a period of stimulated industrial development the increased imports will very likely consist of machinery and plant for the rising industrial establishments; and so far as the money from the hoards has gone abroad to buy such essentials of industrial development, the result is of a kind permanently beneficial to the country. It is also arguable that a protectionist policy might not only bring forth into active circulation money from the old hoards but might further prevent the formation of new hoards by tempting money which might otherwise have been hoarded into industrial enterprise.

It might then be shown that *if* protection can draw away resources from hoards into industrial enterprise the result would be beneficial. But the more important question remains still to be tackled—whether protection can thus draw on hoarded wealth for industrial development. This question leads us to examine a little more carefully the different kinds of hoards. The hoards once belonging to Rajas and big zemindars are already being utilised in our industrial centres. The hoards belonging to the richer agrarians are not likely to be drawn into industries, there being a competitive demand for them from mortgages and other secure investments in the agricultural field where the rate of interest or of usury to be earned is still very large. Then again, hoarding in general has a social and religious side as has so often been emphasised. The increasing prosperity of certain classes in the country has increased the hoarding for social purposes, by the substitution of the yellow metal for the white in the matter of ornaments, which are in a sense a social necessity. Consequently, it cannot be said that protection will draw from hoards a very material proportion of the resources required for industrial development.

Considering generally the nature of capital resources available for industrial development, we have seen above that something is to be expected from a utilisation of the hoards though not much; another potential item consists of agricultural savings but these are not very large nor are they very likely to be diverted to industries; indeed it is not desirable that they should be so diverted. The third potential source consists of the profits of older industries or of nascent industries which are receiving the benefit of protection. This source of capital is of much larger dimensions than the former two, although the capacity of nascent industries for yielding profits and increasing capital are too often exaggerated; indeed such nascent industries will for many years be requisitioning more and more capital from outside in order to attain a scale commensurate with that of their rivals abroad. We thus see the very great importance of foreign capital for the desired industrial development of India on modern lines.

We have now reviewed the arguments advanced by the Commission in favour of protection. The infant industry argument possesses unquestionable theoretical validity; but at the same time protection to nascent industries has to be used judiciously and with discrimination. The rates of protection should be so determined and the protection should be so graduated to the needs of an industry that no room should be left for the complaint that "the infant industries argument sooner or later becomes an argument on behalf of the inefficient producer." It will also be the duty of the Legislature to see that protection on those lines will go to the real infant industries and not to the more influential and powerful but mature industries. As regards the diversified industries argument, we saw that it was in a special measure applicable to Indian conditions. Here again, we have noted that the diversification must be guided by the principle of comparative advantage in national production though that principle need not be interpreted in the usual rigid and static sense. Coming to the wages argument we find that other factors had far more influence on the level of national wages than fiscal policy and that protection could do little in raising that level, although it is not to be denied that in the long period, industrial development reacts on the efficiency of labour and on its remuneration. Both as regards the national wage-level as well as the national revenue any beneficial results of protection are indirect and of a long-period character. Coming to consider the claim that a protectionist policy will improve the revenue resources of the nation, we came to see that in the near future no improvement in revenue position could be expected, unless protectionist duties were kept at a very moderate level so as not to burden the slender resources of the Indian consumer of foreign imports; but if we assume a long period and a successful development of industries due to protection, the taxable wealth of the country might be found to have increased. As regards the potential increase of capital resources to be ascribed to protection, we find that this also is, what the economists would call, a long-period phenomenon.

LECTURE II.

DISCRIMINATING PROTECTION.

It can be fairly claimed for the Report of the Indian Fiscal Commission that in two directions at least its spirit and terminology mark a distinct advance in the history of tariff controversy. For one thing, the Commission did not start by explicitly assuming the merits of any particular fiscal policy as so many other bodies with similar missions have done. Rather, it has analysed pretty exhaustively the arguments for and against the alternative policies before it. Again, the Commission has had the courage to break away from the sway of the usual and time-honoured fiscal shibboleths and has summed its opinions in a memorable and memorisable phrase which is in itself a contribution to the nomenclature of fiscal controversy. The ablest masters of tariff-history like Schmoller and Taussig, have noticed a tendency to compromise in tariff matters supervening on a long and embittered controversy; and the view of the great economists on both sides has been thus happily summarised: "Neither protection nor free-trade is to be blamed, but the misuse of either policy". In another lecture it will be shown that an undue devotion to fiscal catch-words and shibboleths and a tendency to erect economic principles into dogmas characterized only the rank and file of fiscal controversialists on either side. The greatest writer on the free-trade side asserts the existence of valid grounds for intervention by the state to protect industries under proper circumstances. On the other hand the leaders of protectionist thought admit freely that there is no justification for the lengths to which protectionist policy is being carried by the "advanced western countries." This judicious frame of mind is not to be confused with doctrinal eclecticism; rather, it is based on a sense of the necessary limitations of any fiscal policy as well as on the concrete study of facts of national industry.

The phrase which embodies the above point of view—"discriminating protection"—was presented to the Indian Fiscal Commission by the Hon'ble Mr. Harkishenlal when giving his evidence; and, once suggested it became so popular that it became difficult to convince witnesses propounding the most extreme types of views that they were not "discriminators". So united were the suffrages in favour of that type of protection that the dissenting gentlemen agreed to the merits of the formula in spite of their strong reluctance to admit that protection could be subject to any qualifications and limitations.

If one is asked for a description or definition of this "discriminating" protection, the answer is that it is protection based upon and guided by the principle of comparative cost. In other words it extends protection only to such industries as regards which a country enjoys or can be shown to enjoy ultimately a comparative advantage. With this object, the duties are to be such as to place no undue or unnecessary restrictions on the course of foreign trade. Protection is like so many other economic questions a problem in *maxima* and *minima*. The course of trade is to suffer the least possible disturbance in the present with a view to the maximisation of wealth in future. As regards the matter of the fixation of the height of protective duties, guidance is sought partly in the analysis of costs of production at home and abroad, and partly in the elasticity or extensibility of the domestic supply. The protectionist duties are to be removed as soon as the industry in question has developed and has taken its place amongst those low enough on the scale of comparative cost. We thus see that what the Indian Fiscal Commission called "discriminating protection" is based right through on the principle of comparative cost. We have in fact reached the central principle which can guide us aright at all points—as regards the industries to be selected for protection, the extent and measure of assistance to be extended to them, as also the length of the period during which

What is "discriminating" protection?

such help is to be rendered to them. The true task and potentialities of protection are defined by this principle. For the service of protection consists in reducing and attenuating the differences of productive power between countries, so far as these differences are due to differences of industrial phase and of acquired aptitudes. Differences in natural equipment between countries must of course be of a permanent character; but economic supremacy based on mere historical priority as regards the origination of industries is not of an immutable character. Protection can take its share in this task of levelling up, provided it is applied only where there is a prospect of comparative advantage.

Even a slight acquaintance with the protectionist literature will show, that the divergence of theoretical views which marks it is due to the lack of agreement as to such a basic principle. On the one hand, we have the advocates of the "developmental theories" of protection which imply that the "world-economy" is the final and permanent organization; while on the other hand there are the champions of the "defensive theories" who conceive that the national economy is the highest organization to which world-economy relations must continue to be subordinate.* However, from the point of view of the discriminating protectionist there can be no such general or irreconcilable opposition of the national economy and the world-economy, which should rather be conceived of as supplementary to each other. So far as facts can demonstrate that a country can possess a comparative advantage as regards the production of an article, every kind of help—including protectionist duties—should be utilised to secure the particular line of enterprise for the "national-economy"; in all other cases it would be a futile and misspent effort to aggrandize the bounds of national economy at the expense of "world-economy".

The leading features of the scheme of protection formulated

*Cf. Grunzel, *Economic Protectionism*, pp. 152-153.

by the majority might be thus summarised. According to that scheme, protection should be extended only to those industries which possess comparative advantages which will enable them ultimately to face foreign competition without protection. Specially favourable treatment is to be accorded to the industries in which there is a probability that, in course of time, the whole needs of the country could be supplied by the home production. This is equivalent to saying that those industries which possess elasticity of supply in a high degree have special claims to assistance in the shape of protection. It is added that in all cases, the protection contemplated is a temporary protection to be given to industries which will eventually be able to stand alone. Precautions have been recommended to secure the reduction or withdrawal of protection when circumstances justify that course. The rate of protection required by any industry is stated to be what is adequate for the development of the industry—the difference of the relative cost of production in India and foreign countries being indicated as affording some measure of guidance to this adequacy.

Scheme of Protection in the Report.

It is not difficult to show that these conditions are reasonable and necessary. To extend protection to industries which possess no comparative advantage is to deny the very rationale of sane protectionism, which is that protection should divert national resources from the less productive to the ultimately more productive industries. Only such industries as possess natural advantages can fall in the category of ultimately more productive industries. It is also necessary to lay down the condition that protection should be temporary. Perpetual protection would burden the country with a host of parasitic industries. It is difficult to see how such elementary and axiomatic conditions could have struck the gentlemen of the minority as stringent and retarding.

It is easy to find eminent protectionist authorities on

economic science who lay down conditions for the application of protection very similar to those found in the Report. One of the prominent and recent writers on fiscal policy is Fontana-Russo, Professor at the University of Rome. His proposal on the subject deserves to be quoted on account of its remarkable similarity to the views of the majority upon fiscal policy. He asserts that protection might be practised on three conditions:—In the first place, it should be temporary; in the second place, it should be limited to commodities with regard to which, there is comparative advantage; thirdly, protection should be so controlled as to leave no chances of making abnormal profits to local producers. According to the same authority *"the non-observance of any one of these three conditions is equivalent to the grant of special favours to local producers, a privileged position which is contrary to all principles of economic justice"*.* The above-named authority goes on to add a fourth condition that protection should not be extended in any case to raw materials or to "the means of production". In a similar spirit, the Indian Fiscal Commission has laid it down that import duties should not be laid on machinery and that raw materials required for Indian industries should ordinarily be admitted free of duty. This is only reasonable, because import duties on raw materials would nullify the objects aimed at by protectionist measures. Other economic writers can be quoted equally in agreement with the conditions laid down by the majority. The fact is that such conditions are in their nature few and simple. It is difficult to understand what the gentlemen of the minority mean by asserting that "discrimination must vary according to the circumstances for the time being".

Other similar schemes.

Similar conditions and criteria of the application of judicious protection to industries are to be found in numerous protectionist writers. To take another example, Leroy-Beaulieu in his great work would admit to the benefits of protection only such industries as could be expected to be self-supporting. He also

*Fontana-Russo *Traite de Politique Commerciale,* Chap. III.

advises that protective duties should be moderate and should be "concentrated on the fewest objects possible". He is an avowed "discriminator" and he calls his proposed fiscal system "protection with discernment and measure". Another French Economist of note—Landry—has a similar programme. He advocates protection only as regards those articles "which a country can produce profitably"—a phrase which well expresses the notion of comparative advantage. He would have protection consist in "moderately high duties, which must be reduced progressively and are to be abolished at the end of a period of greater or less length".*

"Discrimination" is based on the true scope and limitations of protection.

It can be claimed with truth that the advocates of discriminating protection have correct notions as regards the proper functions, scope and limitations of the efficiency of protection. The highest protectionist authorities agree that protection can only be beneficial in those directions in which a country possesses comparative advantage in protection. Thus Schmoller—one of the greatest of German economists and a master of tariff history—condemns the tendency to exaggerate the potential influence of fiscal policy. He observes that we have come to understand more and more how the economic life of each nation as well as all international trade is based upon certain elementary conditions—conditions which cannot be changed radically by measures whether of the free trade or of protectionist character; on the other hand these basic conditions can countervail, alter, or limit the effects of fiscal policy.† So also Seligman observes that the efficiency of protection at the best is not unlimited. He emphatically lays it down that "Protection must work within the limits of general economic advantages." Unless the artificial environment can be created at a comparatively small cost, it is economically not worth creating.

*Landry, *Manuel d Economique*, pp. 847-848.
†Schmoller, *Volkswirtschaftslehre*, Vol. II, p. 650.

Natural advantages might be trusted in the long run to introduce the proper industries into a country. But this might take a long time; and the function of protection is to guide the productive resources of a country in the direction of these natural advantages and to accelerate the tempo of economic progress in these desirable directions. Here is the true definition of the function and scope of protection. List, the apostle of modern protection, himself argues that it would be folly for a nation to attempt to supply itself by means of national division of labour (i.e. by home production) with articles for the production of which it is not favoured by nature and which it can procure better and cheaper by means of international division of labour (i.e. through foreign commerce).

How discrimination advances the interests of manufacturers.

There are those who sneer at the advocates of discrimination as basing their opinion on the grounds of "concern for the interest of the consumers". But the immediate advantage to the consumer is the least of the reasons for advocating discrimination. Rather discrimination is necessary in the interests of industrial development and progress of the whole country. Indiscriminate protection would abdicate the function of guiding industrial development aright, and would give us an unsound development based upon parasitic industries. As Russo observes, one can approve of this protectionism which accords with the possibility of a definite and durable progress and which has no permanent antagonism with the capacities of different countries. It does not suppress foreign trade and international intercourse but creates new and advantageous conditions of international competition. That author calls such a system "the better form of protectionism" because being based upon natural advantage and comparative costs it does not unduly limit international trade but transforms and develops it.

The guiding principle in the selection of industries for

protection is the principle of comparative cost. The best analysis of the reasoning underlying this selection is to be found in the pages of an American writer on Finance—Professor H. C. Adams: "In case a nation has adopted the theory of protection while at the same time admitting the desirability of an extended international trade, the doctrine of comparative cost may be relied upon to indicate the industries that should be selected for bearing protective duties. It is evident that no amount of protection can within a reasonable time bring an industry which stands high on the scale of comparative cost to the condition of an independent and self-supporting industry. The true policy therefore is to permit the products of such industries to be imported with little or no duty, and to employ these imports as an encouragement for the exportation of those goods that stand low in the scale of comparative cost. Commodities to which the principle of protection may be rationally applied are those which in the matter of cost stand just below the self-sustaining industries. It thus becomes evident that the doctrine of comparative cost does not, as many seem to assume, hold peculiar relations to the theory of free trade; the truth is that nothing but its application can rescue a system of protective duties from becoming an unintelligible mass of unrelated rates." We might go a little further than Professor Adams, and assert that protection granted regardless of that principle would become protection to particular industries at the cost of industrial development in general.

Principle of comparative cost as the basis of all sound fiscal policy.

That the principle of comparative cost is the basic principle of all fiscal policy is made clearer by our observation that even those economists who are apparently reluctant to admit its great theoretical and practical importance, have yet to introduce a paraphrase of it in their treatment of the theory of protection. Thus it is interesting to read what might be called the paraphrase of that principle by such a staunch protectionist as Schuller. According to him the greater the rise in the price of an article due to its production at home the greater is the advantage of free trade in the article to the consumer as compared with its disadvantage to the domestic producer. This is surely equivalent to saying that the greater the difference as regards comparative cost, the smaller is the advisability of the introduction of protection. On the same page Schüller proceeds to emphasize his remark by urging that the greater the difference between the domestic and foreign costs of an article—such difference being in favour of the foreigner—the greater is the advantages resulting from a policy of free-trade. In another place, the same writer warns nations against the evil of extending protectionist duties to "too many articles"; but he suggests no principle or test for selecting the proper number of industries to be selected for protection. Occasionally he observes that the highest principle of fiscal policv is to select that course which brings most advantage to the whole nation. This is very vague; but if it means that fiscal policy should seek to maximise the national dividend then it is perfectly consistent with the principle of comparative cost being made the true index of all judicious fiscal policy.*

Other factors to be considered.

While the law of comparative cost determines the general fitness of an industry for the application of protection, some additional factors have to be taken account of in determining the time suitable for the application of protection to the industry. We have to bear in mind that protection should have something to protect. The industry should at least be in actual existence in the country and not be merely in an embryonic stage. In this connection regard should also be had to the existence or non-existence in the country of the basic industries of which the products are essential for the industry in question. It was very likely owing to these considerations of interconnection of industries and of the principle that protection should have

*Schüller, *Schuzzoll und Freihandel*, pp. 103, 272, 281, 289.

something to protect, that List was for a gradual introduction of protection. In his opinion, in "the case of a nation which contemplates passing from a policy of free competition to one of protection the duties at first must be low, and be graduall increased". It is to be noted that this idea of a gradual introduc tion of protection was placed before the commission by severa witnesses and, among others, by Professor Jevons and Captai Sassoon, a great cotton magnate of Bombay. In an importan sense, protection must needs be gradually introduced since it i only with the development of basic and auxiliary industries tha the serious development of highly technical and complicate industries based on the former can be taken in hand.

In the second place, we have, when inaugurating a prote tionist policy, to look to the stage of economic progress of tl country to which it is to be applied. No economist has striv to emphasise this more than List himself—though we do not nc accept or approve of the particular lines on which he distinguish his stages of economic development. This consideration a points to a fundamental limitations of the potentialities of prot tion. For its useful and fruitful application, a country mu possess a considerable development of capitalism as well as capitalistic organisation and resource. Banking and joint-sto organisation must have gone ahead to furnish the sinews of lar scale industrial enterprise. Marketing organisation and facili of transport must also have developed. List would raise the sc of import duties only *pari passu* with the capital, techni abilities and the spirit of enterprise existing in a nation. fact very strong foundations have to be laid for the structur modern industry. Even in this preparatory stage the state help in the incipient process of industrial development; direct state help to industry—not protection—is the instrume lity fitted for that stage.*

---

*List, *National System of Political Economy* (*translated by S Lloyd*), pp. 248-250.

Looking to the present conditions of our capitalistic and marketing organisation, of our business enterprise and our command over raw materials, one can assert with reason that a policy of discriminating protection is the proper one to adopt in India of to-day. It does not follow from this, however, that our industrial development would have been materially promoted and expedited had the policy of protection been adopted in the earlier days when India had not yet attained these important preliminaries and essentials of industrial progress. It is only natural and patriotic to deplore the decay of the older hand industries of India through the competition of machine-made goods imported from countries where the Industrial Revolution had already made great strides. But it is idle to think that the adoption of protection in those days would have sufficed or contributed to convert the medieval organisation of the country's industries into one adapted to the conditions prevailing in the nineteenth century. Those who have studied the history of the Industrial Revolution in England can appreciate how much preliminary progress in various directions was required before factory industries on modern scale could be started. The immense difficulties of starting manufactures in India in those days are well illustrated by the fate of the European capitalists who came to grief in establishing new industries in India even when state-help was generously extended to them. It is easy to account for their failure. The system of communications was wholly undeveloped, capitalism was in its infancy, while joint-stock enterprise has progressed in India very slowly indeed. For adequate banking development we have been waiting very long, and even now, we are struggling with the financial difficulties of our industrialists and the imperfect organisation of our urban and rural finance. It took many decades to investigate with something like accuracy our mineral resources and our power supplies. It was the great development of Indian export trade in the free-trade era which has raised our credit abroad, supplied us with capital, trained us in business enterprise and organised the production of raw materials on a large scale, so as to meet the potential demand of future great domestic industries ; in the absence of this great development, protection could not have secured the development of a whole system of exotic industries as well as the necessary organisation of commerce and industry. The same view was expressed by Professor R. M. Joshi before the Indian Fiscal Commission. "I do not believe that any particular tariff policy can by itself bring about the economic modernisation of a country, which before the erection of a tariff wall is in a medieval stage of development."

Importance of cost-analysis in fiscal policy.

The Indian Fiscal Commission has chosen the better part in duly emphasising the importance of the relative costs of production in the fixation of tariff rates, while it refused to erect these relative costs into that position of predominant importance to which it has been exalted in some protectionist countries, like America. Assuredly, it would not be advisable to make the differences between costs of production, the sole basis and determinant of tariff-rates. Pushed to its logical consequences, "the principle of equalisation of costs" would annihilate all foreign trade and would burden the consumer with very heavy duties. It would render protection undiscriminating in extent and intolerable in height; it would disregard all considerations of international division of labour and all the great advantages that it stands for. In America the undue application of the principle has resulted in tariff-rates as high as a hundred per cent. and even higher ; indeed stalwarts are not wanting who, like senator Aldrich, "would vote for three hundred per cent. as cheerfully as they would for fifty."

But, properly employed, a study of the relative costs of production is of great value as an element in the judicious determination of rates. Its utility has both a positive and a negative aspect.

Thus, when the difference between the local and foreign costs is found to be very great, it is a *prima facie* proof that we have reached the limits of the advisable employment of protection. Again, a consideration of relative costs will check the exploitation of the consumer and the pursuit of inordinately high profits by the domestic manufacturer under the pretence of industrial development. Where such discriminating fixation of the measure of fiscal duties is absent, both the protection and the resultant profits increase to a dangerous and superfluous degree. It is also to be expected that a careful analysis of the cost of production of an industry and the comparison of local and foreign costs will throw much needed light on the question whether the domestic industry in question deserves protection at all, and whether its inferiority to the corresponding foreign industry is due to what are called "organic" or to "functional" causes. The factors of organic inferiority point to a permanent handicap, while "functional" drawbacks are capable of removal and do not constitute anything like a permanent deficiency in the industrial endowment and equipment of the country. No protection ought to be extended to industries which have been deprived by nature of the necessary "organic" resources. In fact, a thorough-going cost-analysis constitutes the most important part of the organon of the judicious tariff-maker, and is the acid test of the claims advanced by industries to protection. To take an example, it happens very often that industries which have been started in unsuitable localities demand a protection which they ill deserve. A searching analysis of their costs will show that they are weighted by utterly unnecessary elements arising out an unwise choice of locality. Even where a careful study of relative costs cannot fix the rate of protection, it can give us the limit of what the maximum claim for protection should be. As Taussig says, enquiries as to relative cost might not touch the heart of the tariff-problem, and yet "a system of duties really adjusted with care and precision on the basis of cost of production might be expected to help, not only in sharper scrutiny, but in more discriminating judgment on the whole tariff problem".*

Thus, the position of relative costs is in any case one important factor to be considered in the problem of fixing the tariff rates. So difficult indeed is the problem that an authority like List has to admit that such rates "cannot be determined theoretically," and he points rather vaguely to "special conditions as well as relative conditions of industry" as affording some guidance in the matter. But surely, besides these industrial conditions we have to look to some other factors as having a material bearing on tariff rates. One of these consists of revenue considerations for, after all, though the primary objects of a tariff is industrial development, yet finance does not and cannot cease to be one of the important functions of a tariff. And another factor to be taken into account is the capacity of the consumer to bear the burden of a cost of living heightened by the tariff. Both these considerations ought to influence in a special measure the mentality of the tariff-maker in India.

The analysis of cost of production is however one of the most difficult of economic problems and the task of solving it is enough to tax the capacity of the best equipped tariff board. Only a few of the complicating factors of the situation could be referred to here. To start with, we must speak not of a national normal cost of production of an article but of national costs of production. In each industry there are numerous establishments some with high and others with low costs of production. Schaeffle has compared this variety of costs to stratification or to the shading and grading of colours. The causes of this diversity of costs are numerous—varieties of situation and of equipment and differences as regards command of capital, managerial ability, scale of production, etc. The analysis will not be adequate until some kind of average cost or representative

Complexity of the cost-analysis.

*For a masterly study of this problem see Taussig, *Free Trade, the Tariff and Reciprocity*, pp. 134—149.

cost is reached. But apart from this diversity of costs there are difficulties enough to encounter in our analysis. The growth or reduction of the national scale of production also affects the representative or normal cost in the case both of the national industry and of the individual establishment; and one who has to judge of the adequacy or otherwise of protection must take account of such a tendency. Because the increase of the national scale of production and the disappearance of the weaker producing establishment must lower the representative or average cost. Still other factors crowd on us as the cost-analysis proceeds. So far as a business has been successful and cautious in the past a great part of the investment amount is "written off" and hence its costs of production appear abnormally low—but only by a fiction of book-keeping. On the other hand over-capitalisation or "stock-watering" might easily have the effect of abnormally increasing the apparent cost of production of another establishment. The manipulation of the depreciation account also requires careful testing. The wages-bill of each establishment will be affected by alterations in the scale of production while provincial differences of wages have also to be taken into account. In all these matters of changes in costs it is needful to see if the industry is one of increasing or diminishing costs. Finally, the introduction of protection will itself complicate the study of "normal" costs by producing profound changes in the level of prices, wages, interest and rent. Thus with an increase in the demand for capital for industrial development, the rate of interest must go up and hamper that development unless foreign capital is drawn upon.*

Elasticity of domestic supply.

Nor should we leave out of consideration the potentialities of production and the elasticity of the local supply of an article when fixing the import duty on it. Obviously, the article must be capable of responding markedly to the stimulus of the duty if it claims

*An excellent study of the various elements of comparative cost will be found in Schüller's work cited above, at the commencement.

the benefit of the duty, and the greater the elasticity of the local supply the greater the assistance deserved by the industry. On the other hand, it would be in vain to apply protection where the local supply is not capable of marked expansion. No one would suspect Schüller of free-trade susceptibilities, and hence his dicta on the subject are the more noteworthy. His view is that when as the result of the imposition of a duty there has come about a great rise in the price of the dutiable article with only a moderate growth in domestic production, the duty has failed to justify itself. Further ,in general, he advises that duties should be increased only gradually and tentatively, thus obtaining time to study the effect on prices and production.

Adequacy of protectionist duties.

The importance of the adequacy of the protection to be extended to our industries was naturally emphasized by many witnesses before the Commission. It is generally agreed that protection when given should be adequate and the cost analysis and other considerations referred to above are so many indices of the adequacy. But it is to be noted that "adequacy" depends on the conditions prevailing in an industry and we have to consider here the phenomenon of diversity of costs of production in an industry. Protection should be adequate for those establishments of an industry which are well-equipped and judiciously located; but to extend protection so as to make it "adequate" for establishments using obsolete methods and located unwisely is a policy which must ensure stagnation. Protection would fail in its legitimate object if it sought to interfere with the healthy process of the struggle for survival which must go on between the different establishments within the protected industry. The extent of the "natural protection" already enjoyed by local industries in the shape of freights paid by competing imports must also be taken into account before deciding on the adequacy.

The local diversity of costs of production of the same article renders the problem of extending protection to it and of fixing a suitable level of protectionist duties for the article extremely difficult and complicated. It is on this account that even in protectionist literature we meet with a disinclination to the utilization of import duties in such circumstances. Thus it has been argued that the existence of marked disparity of costs of production of an article in a country implies the possibility of extension of production only under unfavourable conditions.

Duration of protective duties.

The last condition prescribed by discriminating protection is the removal of protectionist duties when they have become unnecessary. In the absence of such a provision, the infant industry argument inevitably becomes an argument on behalf of inefficient and parasitic industries on the one hand, or gives unnecessary help to fully developed industries on the other. Again, all protectionist measures must be experimental and tentative in character at the start ; and cases will arise where the initial protection is found on experience to be either unnecessarily large, or, it may be inadequate in amount. The Commission has provided for all these cases and has left the matter to the vigilance and discretion of the Tariff Board. It has wisely refused to set up inelastic, hard and fast time periods for the maturing of industries, in this matter going against the authority of List. Indeed, on this subject—as on some others—List is open to the charge of inconsistency, advocating in one place a gradual diminution of protectionist duties and in a different place an inelastic time limit. Of one thing we might be sure, that the régime of protection in industries is likely to be much longer than those "time-limits" which sanguine industrialists have been imagining or proposing as sufficient. Those who assert that, in a decade or thereabouts, nascent industries could be made self-supporting, are deceiving either themselves, or the public or both. There is nothing in the history of Protection to prepare us for such rapid and decisive industrial victories. Once started on the way, we shall have the duties on our hands for decades, in whatever direction they are extended; for protective duties, even when they are effective, are tonics which require ample time for producing their stimulating effects. Much will, of course, depend on the height of the duties as well as on the natural and functional equipment and preparedness of the protected industry for a successful and prosperous career.

The above description of the desirable type of protection leads us to the question of the possibility of a scientific tariff.

Discrimination as basis of a Scientific tariff.

It has often been argued that protection can never have a scientific character; in the alternative there is the view that the end or object of protection is not a scientific matter, although the actual methods to secure the end —the tariff classification and differentiation—might be capable of rational formulation and defence. It must be admitted, that in actual practice protection almost always tends to degenerate into a selfish scramble. But surely it is not inconceivable that the protectionist could have both a scientific aim and methods. Thus, Professor Pigou has shown that protection might have for its aim and object the maximisation of the national dividend. Professor Carver indicates the theoritical *possibility* of using a tariff to attract labour and capital to industries which are more productive from the social point of view. The ideal of a well-balanced industrial system is also a scientific one. It is no more unscientific to propound a system of exceptions to free-trade that it is to set forth a set of exceptions to the system of freedom of contract. The older school of free-traders held the doctrine of comparative cost in a highly rigid and statical sense. But it is now recognized by the highest authority that comparative advantages, in industries and industrial leadership, are dynamic phenomena and possess a changing and shifting character. As Dr. Marshall remarks, "the percentage of the world's trade which is governed by differences in natural resources is increasing, while that which is governed by differences of industrial phase, and of aptitude for particular sorts and grades of manufacture, is less now than formerly." It is in this transformation that protection of a judicious character can play a part, and the forwarding of such a transformation is its true aim. As regards the methods of discriminating protection, they are scientific as long as the working of protection is, as shown above, kept consistent with the principle of comparative costs.

Discrimination not a matter of mere procedure.

It has been argued that while "protection" is a matter of policy, "discrimination" is a question of procedure only, and that consequently by emphasizing the importance of discrimination the vital issue of the problem is obscured. With all deference, it can be answered that while discriminating protection is a well-recognised principle in economic literature, there is no economist of importance who will subscribe to the principle of unqualified and indiscriminate protection. Indeed, the latter can hardly be dignified with the name of a principle; and if the choice lay between complete free-trade and an all-round protection, few would be found to vote for the latter. It is not protection in any shape or form that is to be welcomed but protection of the proper type; not that protection which enables the manufacturer to exploit the consumer, which helps the rise of trusts and cartels, which burdens the consumer needlessly; but that right type of protection which extends help to the proper industries, in the necessary measure and for the requisite period of time. It would be easy to quote the authority of eminent economists on this point, but the lecture on the "Verdict of the Economists" is the proper place for such dicta. It is permissable, however, to quote the late Mr. Gokhale and to throw the weight of his authority into the scale of discriminating protection: "The right kind of protection is that under which the growing industries of a country receive the necessary stimulus and encouragement and support that they require, but under which care is taken that no influential combinations, prejudicial to the interests of the general community, come into existence. The wrong kind of protection, on the other hand, is that under which powerful influences and combinations and interests receive assistance to the prejudice of the general community, the general tax-payers of the country. And I believe that the right kind of protection, if available, will do good to India". It is to be noted that the great economist and publicist of India emphasized the desirability—not so much of protection—as of the right type of protection.

Other objection considered.

On this subject a further contention of the minority of the Indian Fiscal Commission is that "dicrimination must vary according to the circumstances for the time being". It is difficult to understand how the principles of discrimination can be imagined as varying from time to time. The truth of the matter is that the main condition to be considered in extending protection is the presence of natural advantages in the case of the industry; all other conditions are either of a subsidiary character or of the nature of corollaries of the main condition. That being so, one cannot understand how discrimination can vary from time to time. Do the gentlemen of the minority imply that a time will ever come when we shall be profitably employed in bolstering up industries which possess no natural advantages? Of course, the circumstances to which the principles of discriminating protection have to be applied do vary, and as a consequence the range and height of duties will also fluctuate.

Adverse comment has been elicited by the observation of the Majority Report, that as a result of the policy of discriminating protection "India for many years to come it likely to concentrate on the simpler forms of manufactured goods". It would be unjust and preposterous to assert that the majority of the Indian Fiscal Commission were framing a special policy with the set design of producing such a result; rather they expressed their apprehensions that whatever was the fiscal policy adopted, it could not be expected that in a short time India should develop the most highly complicated and technically advanced industries. The reasons for this fear are obvious. Our basic industries are yet undeveloped and it takes several decades to bring them to maturity. Again, a great number of auxiliary industries must also have progressed far before the more complicated industries are taken in hand. The industrial history of all nations show that progress towards elaborate manufactures must be gradual. Those who find this a hard saying are reminded of Dr. Marshall's view that a country which is new to modern industrialism has "to win elementary victories over nature. Her free capital is seldom equal to the urgent demands for it, which are made by industries of agriculture and transport ; and therefore, vigorous as her people may be individually, she has little opportunity for pioneering the more complex methods of industry in advance of older countries, which have abundant capital and energy free for such works." (Marshall, Industry and Trade, p. 105).

Arguments from "national self-sufficiency."

Such being the position of the discriminating protectionist it might be asked what he has got to say as regards the idea of national self-sufficiency—at least as regards the military requirements of a country—on which stress has been laid by quite a number of advocates of protection. Now, coming to analyse the notion of national self-sufficiency we find that it might mean one of two things. In the first place there is the idea of complete national independence in the economic sphere—what has been called "Autarkie" by continental economists. This ideal—if indeed it can be so called —is an impossible one. No one with any claim to scientific distinction has advanced such a project ; for as Schmoller observes :—"no civilised state, and none of the smaller states in particular can avoid trade dealings with other countries". Indeed, in spite of the very heavy tariffs of our age, internatonal trade has grown by leaps and bounds. That fact indeed has been gloried in by certain protectionist writers, and attempts have been made to give the credit of the movement to protection, on the supposition that such a policy increases the activity of a country in world-trade. At the best however such a claim is an exaggeration. It omits the leading factors influencing the expansion of world-trade ; these factors consist of the increased volume and variety of both production and consumption among nations. Fiscal policy does affect these phenomena but to a much smaller extent than is generally believed. It can be easily seen that a policy of economic self-sufficiency in the larger sense is entirely incompatible with the great growth of our export and import trade and with the ambition to develop, at any rate, the export trade much further.

We now come to consider the more reasonable aspect of the theory of national self-sufficiency. It is argued that protection should be employed to initiate and preserve those industries without which the existence of the state would be in danger, and in particular those which produce the apparatus and essentials of war. There is no doubt that the experience of the last war has greatly reinforced the strength of the argument for military preparedness on the part of nations ; it is the duty of every nation to insure itself against a *debacle* in the next war. While admitting all this, however, it should not be forgotten that there are many different ways—and not one only—of effecting such insurance. Discrimination has to be exercised among these various methods; and then we shall see that the problems of preparedness against war and of protection are not identical but can be kept separate. No doubt, in the case of some of the essential industries protection is desirable, such industries being those in which the attainment of a position of comparative advantage can be looked for at least in the future. There are other industries as regards which the possibilities of a nation becoming a considerable producer are so remote that the payment of bounties, on the essential scale of production, constitutes a smaller burden than the imposition of protectionist duties.

The burden caused by bounties is limited by the desired scale of production while that due to import duties hits every consumer of the article. There are further alternatives, of the state itself producing the urgently required quantity of the article, in question, in Government factories, and of the "purchase and accumulation by the Government of a large fixed stock or reserve". The above course of reasoning emphasises the recommendation of Professor Taussig to the effect that general arguments for protection should be kept separate from specific arguments for military preparedness.*

Evils of indiscriminate and uncontrolled protection.

In concluding this lecture, it is interesting to contrast with the principles and methods of discriminating protection as described above, the objects and working of indiscriminate and unqualified protection. The latter burdens the consumer needlessly by raising prices all round, even in the case of those articles which cannot be successfully produced locally, either at all or for a long time to come. It abdicates the function of true protection—which is to guide production in the relatively more profitable and productive channels exclusively. It wastes the available capital and resources of the nation in experiments, many of which must end in failure, because of the absence of natural advantages in those particular directions. As it is, Indian capital and productive resources are not adequate to the great task of industrial development, and we can ill-afford to squander them in unprofitable directions. It should also be remembered that nothing succeeds like success. If many of the earlier and indiscriminate industrial experiments end in failure, the hands of the clock of progress will be set back. On the other hand, discriminating protection will start only promising industries of which the success will be highly probable ; and such success will lead not only to the encouragement of further industrial enterprise but also to the ac-

*Taussig, *Free Trade, the Tariff and Reciprocity*, p. 199.

cumulation of capital, experience and organising power which will be helpful in all succeeding efforts. Finally, indiscriminating protection will considerably reduce our import trade—a result which will have an unfavourable influence on our export trade as well as on production in general. The views of a Danish economist Dr. Birck, Professor in the University of Copenhagen, on the subject of discriminating protection deserve to be mentioned here:—"Protection must not be too general, and must be limited to a few trades, as it is only an exception that a large part of the productive forces of the country are unemployed. A uniformly adjusted duty on all goods or 'solidarity protection' may be compared to Baron Munchausen's attempt to lift himself by his pigtail, and the only effect will be increased prices."*

Those who are unaccustomed to economic discipline will perhaps express their impatience with a protectionist system hedged round by proper qualifications and discrimination. To such the answer could be given that all wise fiscal policy should be guided at once by sound theory and by the lessons of tariff history. Professor Marshall has spoken of "the cumbrous qualifications of the free-trade position" ; but it has further to be noted that as a policy, free-trade is simplicity itself compared to protection. An efficient system of protection is a scientific affair and not a matter of easy shibboleths and generalisations or of facile dogmatism.

---

*Birck, *Marginal Theory of Value*, p. 261.

LECTURE III.

THE VERDICT OF THE ECONOMISTS.

"Your sages, just the men to shrink
From the gross weights, coarse scales and labels broad
You offer their refinement."

Browning: *Men and Women.*

In the case of long standing economic controversies, in the course of which appeals have been constantly made to the popular tribunal for support and approval, there is a temptation "to compress economic principles into dogmas", and to set forth doctrines in the form of creeds. The age-long controversy as regards protection and free-trade forms no exception to this undesirable tendency. Fortunately that tendency is confined to the rank and file on both sides—to the minor lights and leaders. The great masters of fiscal doctrines have too much breadth of view and moderation to believe that shibboleths, catchwords and labels designed for popular appeal could be made to comprehend the immense complexities of economic life, and they have recognised the danger of formulating their teaching into opposed and antithetical dogmas. The present tendency in all the leading exponents of the various schools is in the direction of being guided by "the ascertained facts of concrete industry in deciding—in a spirit of judicious discrimination—how far any particular industry deserves to be assisted and encouraged by the State, whether by protectionist import duties or by other measures".

Marshall.

The balanced judgment of the *doyen* of English economists is reflected in his opening dictum on the subject of fiscal policy in his latest work:—"Nearly every sort of fiscal policy works some good and some evil. Whether the good or the evil preponderates depends much on the adaptation of policy to the conditions of industry and trade in the country affected; and on the foresight, breadth of vision and ability with which it is developed". Overstatements of arguments whether for free-trade or protection are to be condemned, as well as the tendency shown by some economists to "compress economic principles into dogma." Much harm has been done by the formulation of economic precepts or theorems without due qualifications, and as Dr. Marshall says, "in the long run it might has been better both for England and for free-trade, if they (the older English economists) had been compelled to make prominent those cumbrous qualifications which they omitted." The case for protection is thus, not a general one, but one dependent upon the favourable potentialities of intervention by the state on behalf of infant industries, where the particular circumstances of time and place are suitable. Both the qualifications of the general case for free-trade and the advisability of protection in particular directions depend upon a discriminating analysis of these circumstances.

The infant industry argument receives due support and recognition from Dr. Marshall. He censures some of the older economists for failing "to allow for the special circumstances of the new countries" and for using as convertible the two phrases —"the commodities which a country can now produce most easily," and "the commodities which a country has the greatest potential advantages for producing." This consideration lies at the base of the infant industry argument and forms a valid "ground for intervention by the state in favour of nascent manufactures under the particular circumstances of time and place." To a certain extent, the case for state-assistance to infant industries is strengthened where these industries have "latent powers of economy through production on a large scale", because, among other things, the price of the product of such industry, and consequently the burden to the consumer, is not likely to increase by the full amount of the duty. Nevertheless, as Dr. Marshall warns us, these considerations cannot legitimately lead to any sort of general rule in favour of extending protection to industries conforming to Increasing Return. Due regard is to be had to the different kinds of economies of massive production, only some which can be developed by the use of protection, as well as to the fact that tariff help to one such industry might conceivably hinder the progress of a number of other similar industries. This careful interpretation by Dr. Marshall of the old argument for assistance to infant industries in new or backward countries in supplemented by a felicitous remark as regards the connotation of the expression "new countries"— "A country, which has been regarded as old, may become in fact new almost suddenly, for the great body of its people may awake to the attractions of modern industrial methods; and apply them energetically to rich natural resources, which have hitherto lain almost dormant. Japan has become new in this sense during the present generation; India, China, Siberia and even Brazil, with much larger natural resources may become new ere the present century has passed."

In his latest work on "*Money, Credit and Commerce,*" Dr. Marshall has a section on "Import duties favouring a nascent industry." In the course of these remarks he has on the one hand sharpened the edge of the infant industry argument, while on the other hand he has emphasized anew the need for discrimination in the use of such duties. These duties are to be used in the case of young industries in undeveloped countries and only "*when no other means are available for bringing national resources to the aid of a particular backward industry.*" Such duties, it is added, must inevitably do some hurt to those national industries which are manufacturing for exportation. But, on the balance, the country might gain by the employment of these duties, "for the energy developed in a few high-class progressive industries may spread over a great part of the industrial system of the country, just as an iron screen, which concentrates the whole draught of a chimney on a small part of a nascent fire, may generate an intense local heat, which spreads and pioneers the way for a broad, strong fire."

The case for diversification of industries in backward countries has also been emphasized by Dr. Marshall, and the social and generally educative effects have been lucidly pointed out. Thus, he observes that "a new country may be dominantly rural ; may lack the stimulus and culture of a nervous town life, and have no access to the economies of manufacture on a large scale ; she will then derive comparatively little consolation from knowing that there are busy hives of industry and thought in remote lands." Protective tariffs, remarks Dr. Marshall in another place, might "increase the manufacturing population relatively to the agricultural, and thus develop centres of complex and various social life and high culture, and provide an ever-widening choice of occupations for people of varying temparaments and capacities." The case for diversification of industry could not have been put more comprehensively or felicitously. On the other hand, Dr. Marshall does not fail to draw our attention to certain *necessary deductions from the advantages* of diversification of industries carried out by the instrumentality of tariffs. Such tariffs in favouring manufactures must needs "hinder the development of the agricultural resources of the country. This involves some retardation of the growth of commercial centres ; which are nearly, though not quite, as important from the social point of view as the industrial centres." On the whole, it would appear that, even after making allowance for this latter circumstance, there is "a valid, but not a strong, ground for intervention by the State" with the object of the diversification of national industries.

So far we have seen that there are valid grounds in particular cases for the employment of tariffs, in order to secure industrial development in certain directions. Such utilisation of tariffs must be of a discriminating character, and with a due regard to the concrete facts of the conditions of industry and trade in a country. In general, also, the case for the employment of tariffs is much stronger in backward and new countries. Thus, we read in the valuable contribution of Dr. Marshall to *"After War Problems"* that "for two generations it has been clear that some of the pleas of Indian industries for protection are stronger than any which could be put forward for British industries." Nor even in the case of the advanced manufacturing countries like Great Britain, is it denied that there exist "some new strong arguments in favour of a limited protection to a few industries." On the other hand Dr. Marshall draws attention to items on the other side of the account. "Such aid when given in the form of Protective duties, is seldom free from serious indirect evils, economic, political and moral." The conscientious student of Economics as well as the wise legislator, must keep before him both the benefit which a judicious protectionist policy can bring, and the potentialities of those indirect evils which can be minimised only by the wisest statesmanship. We in India must benefit by the warning given by the tariff history of so many countries. The experience of many protectionist countries in that direction has also been summarised for us by the same great author:—"I found that, however simple the plan on which a protective policy started, it was drawn on irresistibly to become intricate; and to lend its chief aid to those industries which were already strong enough to do without it. In becoming intricate it became corrupt and tended to corrupt general politics."

Schmoller.

With Schmoller we come to another point of view—that of the Historical school of Germany. Schmoller has the best right to speak as the representative of this school. In his great work on "Foundations of Economics" he lays down the well-balanced dictum that "neither free-trade nor protection is to be blamed but the misuse of either and the employment of either policy under unsuitable circumstances." The same spirit breathes in his observation, that "to-day we do not see any more a question of principle between free-trade and protection ; rather both are to be regarded as two alternative instrumentalities for carrying out the aims of true fiscal policy."* He condemns what he calls the neo-mercantilism which has inspired the protectionist policy of the western countries ; but he rejoices that in spite of this bias we are coming to—and indeed have not departed from—"a compromise between the two systems which is very necessary. No modern state has practised absolute free-trade; and none has cut itself off completely from free-trade." He feels the atmosphere being cleared and men becoming more far-sighted than before, because they have experienced "the hardships and evils of high protective duties." He believes that in the near future we shall have a less disturbed condition of civilization accompanied by "a more free-trade epoch."* The ideas at the root of both movements—high protection and the economic exploitation of the weaker nations—are connected, and both will gradually disappear.

While Schmoller is an advocate of moderate protection, he never loses sight of the due scope and limited functions of protection. "Gradually the false and exaggerated claims, of both the protectionist and the free-trader—but particularly of the former—about the influence of fiscal measures are being reduced."* This is because, as Schmoller puts it, we are recognising more and more that there are fundamental facts in the economic life of every nation which no fiscal policy—whether protectionist or free-trade—can easily change, if indeed at all. Again, we know that any scheme of fiscal policy can be brought to naught by such facts. The causes of the progress of trade are many and complicated, and among them fiscal policy is only one and often it forms by no means the most important of these causes. If the purely

---

*Schmoller, *op. cit* vol. II, pp. 647-648.

Ib. p. 651.

economic causes, says Schmoller, are present in a marked degree, trade must go ahead inspite of obstructions put in its way by protection, whereas a poor country has no great export and import trade in spite of its free-trade policy. Nevertheless, he argues that it is only natural that a free-trade policy should be a stimulus to the growth of commerce, while the protectionist policy must have the opposite tendency.

It is interesting to note how Schmoller disposes of many of the popular arguments for protection. Thus the argument urged by some American writers that protection can raise wages or maintain them high against the competition of those countries in which low wages prevail is characterised by Schmoller as "Pharisaic"; for his part he cannot see that protection is likely either to raise or lower wages.* He is also opposed to the argument about "autarkie"—national self-sufficiency to be secured through protection. He denies that any civilized state could, or should, avoid trade relations with other states. One can, of course, on the other hand think of making one's country independent of others in the matter of those products of which the deprivation would mean death. Many German economists had laid great stress upon tariff as a weapon of negotiation (Machtsmittel). Schmoller is against the exaggerations of this argument. He points out that these weapons have been very often used unskilfully and consequently without effect.

But even more instructive than Schmoller's arguments is his great historical review of the effects and characteristics of protection in different countries. Beginning with Russia, he shows that with a more moderate system of protection, her manufactures would have developed more slowly, but on sounder lines; the subjects would not have been crushed under taxes, the state would not have been burdened with such a heavy debt, nor need all strata of economic Russia have been so

---

**Ib.* p. 650.

thoroughly corrupted through the action of capitalism."* In that country the fiscal policy of protection was pursued at the cost of an agricultural population which formed 83 per cent. of the Russian nation, and for the benefit of a small minority of industrialists, merchants and officials. In the case of the tariff policy of the United States, the observations of such a great historian of fiscal policy are no less instructive:—"The great question of the future is whether the money-maker or the respectable and farsighted citizen will get the upper hand in future. On the solution of this question depends the result whether protection is likely to be reduced to a reasonable degree and measure." As regards France, it is noted that under the protectionist system France has failed to attain a brilliant evolution, but has rather reached a stationary and quiet stage, both as regards her agriculture and industry. Her industries made little progress until 1898, and even since have not taken much part in the forward world movement. Her commerce cannot be said to have been destroyed by her protectionist policy, but neither has it been stimulated thereby.

Naturally, we are most interested in hearing what Schmoller has to say about protectionism in Germany. He is so far a protectionist, that he approves of the introduction of protection by Bismarck as a "necessary and wholesome change," but even Bismarck does not remain his hero for long, since "after 1885 he fell into the aggressive mentality of old mercantilism." Consequently, Schmoller approves whole-heartedly of the reduction of the German tariff under Caprivi, which was indeed necessary, if Germany "was not going to lose a great part of her tolerably stable export trade". He condemns the conduct of the protectionist party in bringing about the fall of Caprivi; nor has he a good word to say of the more recent German tariffs "which roused the hopes of the extreme protectionists" and "raised the tariff in many directions needlessly." As a

---

**Ib.* p. 644.
Ib. p. 626.

scientific protectionist, he could see little to approve of in the parliamentary manœuvres which precede the formation of tariffs. "The deliberations in the Reichstag were a fresh proof of the very limited capacity of great parliaments to construct tariffs wisely."

The place which List occupies in the history of protection is so important that no apology is needed for discussing here the leading features of his protectionist system. Moreover, as is well-known, Ranade drew his inspiration from List in initiating the work of the protectionist school in India. In his sense, List was present at the birth of Indian protectionism, and now that the country is about to change the lines of its tariff policy, it might be well to analyse the teaching of List in order to derive lessons applicable to our present conditions.

List.

List is open to the general charge of exaggeration in his historical and theoretical treatment of his subject. Nevertheless, the advocate of indiscriminate protection will find little support in his writings. Indeed most of his so-called followers have little right to invoke his name. If List came to life again he would be surprised to find a great system of agrarian protection instituted by his followers—he himself was a pronounced opponent of protection to agriculture. Many conditions of, and limitations to the employment of protection which he defined and laid down, are being systematically neglected by many who, therefore, take his name in vain. It can be easily shown that List was a discriminating protectionist of the most pronounced type. In the first place, it is to be noted that he recommended the extension of protection only to such industries in the country as possess natural advantages. Thus, he observes:—" It would be folly for a nation to attempt to supply itself by means of national division of labour (*i.e.*, by home production) with articles for the production of which it is not favoured by nature, and which it can procure better and cheaper by means of international division of labour (*i.e.*, through foreign commerce)." He has also a true perspective of the development of national manufactures; consequently he does not recommend protection even to all promising manufactures straightaway. He knows that it takes a long time for a nation, even under a protectionist regime, to prepare itself for the development of the finer and more finished manufactures. He would therefore postpone the extension of protection to the finer grades of manufacture to a suitable time. " Protection is only beneficial to the prosperity of a nation so far as it corresponds with the degree of the nation's industrial development. *Every exaggeration of protection is detrimental ;* nations can only obtain a perfect manufacturing power by degrees. On that account also, two nations which stand at different stages of industrial cultivation, can with mutual benefit make reciprocal concessions by treaty in respect to the exchange of their various manufacturing products." Again, in the case of countries which have not yet reached an advanced stage of industrial development, he would allow "all complicated machinery to be imported free of duty, or at least only levy a small duty upon them, until they themselves are in a position to produce them as readily as the most advanced nations. Machine manufactories are in a sense the manufactures of manufactories and every tax on the importation of foreign machinery is a restriction on the internal manufacturing power." The Indian Fiscal Commission has adopted this recommendation in its treatment of machinery. In view of the present-day demand for protection to key industries, it is interesting to note that in the opinion of List the proper way of extending help is not by means of import duties. "The state should at least encourage and directly support its home manufactories of machinery, so far as their maintenance and development may be necessary to provide at the commencement of a time of war, the most necessary requirements, and under a longer interruption by war, to serve as patterns for the erection of new machine factories."*

It needs to be properly emphasized that List recommended very strongly a *gradual introduction of protection, beginning with very moderate duties.* This aspect of List's teaching has been so constantly neglected by his would-be followers, that some of his dicta on the subject might be quoted with advantage— "If the manufacturing power to be protected be still in the first period of its development, the protective duties must be very moderate ; they must only rise gradually with the increase of the mental and material capital, of the technical abilities and spirit of enterprise of the nation. Neither is it at all necessary that all branches of industry should be protected in the same degree." In other places he also observes that the protectionist duties imposed at first must be low, and be gradually increased,......in the ratio in which capital, technical abilities, and the spirit of enterprise are increasing in the nation or are being attracted to it from abroad."*

There are other lessons which we in India can derive from the writings of List besides that of the importance of discrimination in the use of protection. He advised countries "always to favour the importation of productive power"—and in particular of foreign capital. The success of protection, according to him, depended mainly on the circumstance " that by the policy of favouring native manufacture a mass of foreign capital, mental as well as material, is attracted into the country."* For the nationalisation of foreign capital he relied upon industrial development within the country. Finally, it is to be noted that List did not rely exclusively upon protection as the means of national development. He had the true perspective of the larger programme of national development in which protection was only one of the factors.

---

*List, *op. cit.*, pp. 131 ; 259-260 ; 252.
*List, pp. 144-145 ; 249-250.
*List, pp. 294 ; 183.

Since America is the classical home of protection ,and has had the longest and most instructive experience of protectionist policies, it is most important to refer to the views of the great historian of the tariffs of that country. Dr. Taussig—Professor of Economics at Harvard and sometimes Chairman of the United States Tariff Commission—is famous alike for his contributions to economic theory and to tariff history. The position taken up as regards the tariff controversy by a person of his eminence and research must be of considerable interest to all students of economic doctrines ; and fortunately Prof. Taussig has taken them into his confidence by publishing a number of valuable papers in his volume on Free-trade and the Tariff. In his brilliant essay on 'the cost of production and the Tariff' he thus sums up his position as regards the fiscal controversy: "I would not have the reader infer that I am an unqualified free-trader . . . . The case in favour of free-trade has indeed always seemed to me *prima facie* strong ; and prolonged investigation and reflection have served to confirm me in this opinion. But it is only a *prima facie* case. There may be off setting advantages which rebut the presumption." He differs from the German Historical School of which the leaders assert that there is no question of principle involved in the controversy, and that it is all a matter of advantage or disadvantage in any given case. Prof. Taussig's view, on the other hand, is that while the fundamental principle of free-trade has been little shaken, we have to take account of a great many qualifications. The practical result is that "few economists now-a-days would say that there is one good tariff policy, and one only applicable to all countries and all conditions"—a dictum strikingly similar to the one from Dr. Marshall which claimed our attention a short while ago. We must now consider these "qualifications" of free-trade or in other words the valid arguments for protection. In the case of Dr. Taussig the chief emphasis is laid upon the young industries argument, which

Taussig.

according to him, is not only applicable to backward and new countries but which "points to some possibilities of ultimate gain", even in the case of developed industrial countries. The argument from diversification of industries under protection does not appeal to the same author, at least in the case of the advanced nations ; but he admits the force of the allied "political and social arguments as to the avoidance of extremes." Protection is also legitimately utilised to prevent undue fluctuations in industry, for example, those caused by dumping of a temporary nature. On the other hand he asserts that "no economist of standing would maintain that a protective tariff is the one decisive factor in making a country's rate of wages high."

But the most valuable observations of Prof. Taussig have been made in connection wtih the painstaking and brilliant investigation which he has instituted as regards the influence of protection on American industries. The first important generalisation is that no amount of protection can lead to success in the absence of comparative advantage as regards the industry in question. This, for example, is the explanation of the complete failure of tariff to develop the production of raw silk, or of some branches of woolen manufactures, under the regime of protection in America. The same factor has influenced the fate of protection afforded to beet sugar. The practical corollary of this principle is the recognition of the limitation of the potentialities of protectionist policies, and the advisability of their discriminating application only in those directions where comparative advantage exists. Prof. Taussig urges that the principle of comparative advantage is indispensable for explaining the international trade of any country and the working of its tariff policy. It is perhaps needless to emphasise that the recognition of the principle of comparative advantage is the basis of all discriminating protection.

Another of the valuable generalisation of Prof. Taussig is that "the external commercial policy of a nation is among the least of the causes to which it owes its progress". In a sense, indeed, this is only a corollary of the principle of comparative advantage, since protection can succeed only when applied within the limits fixed by that principle. This does not mean of course, that protection is of no value in causing industrial development, if applied wisely and with discrimination. It has a guiding function, as Prof. Taussig observes in discussing the influence of protection on the American iron industry, and he asks, "Would these forces have turned in *this direction* so strongly and unerringly but for the shelter from foreign competition." He shows that the stimulus from great profits due to protection promotes the unhesitating investment of capital in the particular direction. But for protection, in the case of that industry, "profits would have been lower ; and possibly the progress of investment, the exploitation of the natural resources, even the advance of the technical arts would have been less keen and unremitting." We take it then that the function of judicious protection is to increase the rapidiy of the development of industry provided it starts with comparative advantage. More cannot be claimed for protection. Prof. Taussig clinches this by showing that within the United States under a regime of the most absolute free-trade, there has been a gradual and steady growth of manufactures in regions that a few decades ago were exclusively agricultural. Hence his well-founded belief that "the general structure and spirit of the social body are much more important than specific encouragement to this or that industry." He adds elsewhere that "the dependence of our manufacturing industries on tariff duties is enormously exaggerated."

As might be expected, Professor Taussig, like Schmoller, is for the general reduction of the present high tariffs in so many countries. Regarding the American tariffs since 1890 he observes that "few economists would say a good word for such an exaggerated protectionist policy, one so intolerant of foreign competition and foreign supply." He saw with satisfaction before the war that the outlook was "for a moderation of extreme protectionist policy." While not approving as a theorist of the principle of basing tariffs on costs of production, he acknowledged that it might have a moderating influence and that it "might be expected to help not only in sharper scrutiny but in more discriminating judgment on the whole tariff problem."

In these days, when we are hearing so much of protection to key industries and industries of war munitions, it is very instructive to hear the view of Prof. Taussig on the subject. He admits that the strictly economic arguments for protection have been reinforced by the hard facts of the international conflict. But as regards the manufacture of essential articles for the civilian population (the key industries), he would ask whether even protection is likely to make countries self-sufficing; also whether protection to these industries would not hurt other industries. Speaking generally, whether about war munitions or other essentials, he lays down a useful rule of practical compromise :— Complete dependence on the foreigner is not conceivable for a great nation; but absolute self-sufficiency is not necessarily the wisest policy. He would keep apart arguments for protection and arguments for military preparedness as far as possible. Protectionist duties are only one means of securing the needed supply of munitions and essential articles at the proper time; there are other instrumentalities which might be utilised—bounties on production, government purchase at guaranteed prices, and the accumulation by the government of the necessary stocks or reserves.

Arnauné.

Just as Prof. Taussig has garnered for us the results of the protectionist policies of America, so the recent work of Prof. Arnaune has furnished us with lessons derived from the fiscal policy followed by France during half a century. He finds faults with the high tariff of France, because its authors have been so busy putting obstacles in the way of imports, that they have failed to see the indirect consequence of their policy—the diminution of exports. The French protectionists in a word, are so pre-occupied with the affairs of the domestic market that "they are resigned to the diminution of the foreign markets for French goods." Then again, according to the same author, French protection is of an indiscriminating character and has gone too far in giving protection to industries producing raw materials:* Thus France has extended protection to iron, steel and coal industries. Consequently, the costs of production have become very unfavourable in France for other industries. The agriculturist as well as the industrialist has to pay a higher price for such instruments and machinery as he uses. On the other hand, the metallurgical industries also have to bear the duties on coal. Arnaune complains that the French system of protection is not based upon any general principle; but that the state is absorbed in the task of promoting the particular interests of individual industries without due regard to the effects of the policy on the national economic condition as a whole. The fact is, that unless the policy of protection is guided by the principle of comparative advantage in production, it becomes a collection of unconnected and incoherent import duties. It becomes a system of trying to help individual industries even at the cost of the industrial system as a whole. Indiscriminating protection, in effect, takes away with one hand what it gives with the other.

Leroy Beaulieu.

It is no matter of surprise that under these circumstances French economists are emphasising the necessity of manipulating protection "with discernment and measure". It is a welcome variant of our expression "discriminating protection", supplied by a master like Leroy Beaulieu. It is interesting to know the idea of "protection with discernment and measure" formulated by such a writer; what he wants is free-trade ultimately, but under the existing circumstances, "a liberal fiscal system which should

---

*Arnaune, *Commerce Exterieur*, pp. 532; 497; 517.

tend more and more to facilitate international trade and connections." This expression does not imply that customs duties should not be utilised for revenue purposes or even within proper limits for protection; but as the distinguished author says, the precept "aims at their moderation and at their concentration upon the fewest possible objects".* He goes on to observe that no country should attempt to initiate industries which, "under the local circumstances cannot take strong roots but which are likely to remain rickety and artificial" If any exceptions are to be made to this rule, they can only be based on the grounds of national defence, and should be adopted only after very careful examination. Moreover, it is absurd for any country to attempt to be self-sufficing and to produce all articles. On the contrary, the industrialisation of countries should be based upon the principle of international division of labour and of the immense advantages, both direct and indirect, which flow from it. Further, Leroy Beaulieu goes on to remark, that it is not enough for those who desire to secure protection for an industry merely to show that it exists or that it can exist in the country. It should be further demonstrated that the country has the right measure of aptitude for the development of the industry in question.

Schüller.

It is well to conclude the present study by examining the views of Schüller—an able protectionist writer from Austria, who has established a reputation in recent years by his writings on the fiscal question. As a theorist, Schüller has deserved well by a careful analysis of costs of production as affecting fiscal theory. He has further contributed some vigorous criticism of the naïve free-trade theory, and has expended much ingenuity in trying to show how through the importation of commodities susceptible of domestic production, the sum-total of domestic

---

*Leroy-Beaulieu, *Traite Theorique et Pratique d' Economie Politique*, Vol. IV., pp. 103—104.

production is diminished and economic life is impaired. There can be no doubt, that in working out these theories Schüller rather exaggerates the less favourable aspects of free-trade. A new turn is given by him to the doctrine of comparative costs as the criterion of national superiority in the matter of production. In the first place, according to him, we have to compare the costs of production both abroad and at home; the greater the difference in this respect in favour of the foreign source of supply the weaker is the case for protection. In the second place, he would note the difference between the various sets of domestic costs—in particular those corresponding to different scales of production; the smaller the difference in this respect, the stronger is the presumption in favour of protection. In fact, Schüller disavows the doctrine of comparative cost in the older form only to re-admit it in another shape. A more realistic appearance is no doubt given to the older doctrine by taking into account the diversity of costs both at home and abroad, but the added complications do not seen to be favourable to clarity of thought. At the conclusion of his analysis, he is left with the rather vague formula that protection should be resorted to only where the sum total of national interests require its application.

One cannot help noting a remarkable contrast between the theoretical views of Schüller and his practical proposals. On the theoretical side he is an aggressive champion of protection; he rejects the theory of comparative costs as formulated by the older economists; he is opposed to the "Developmental theory of protection," because of its negativing the possibilities of perpetual protection ; and he censures List for the limitations and restrictions the latter is constantly introducing. Nevertheless the whole aspect of Schüller changes very abruptly when he passes from his theoretical work to a consideration of the prevailing system of protectionism. The fourth and the seventh chapters of his work on *"Schuzzoll und Freihandel"* which deal at length with the shortcomings of the present system of protection as exemplified in different countries will amply repay a careful study. According to him, none of these tariff systems have been constructed in the interests of the nation as a whole. The interests of the consumers have always been sacrificed to those of the organized mass of producers. But even amongst producers generally, those gain the most by protection, which require it least—the stronger producers being subsidised by protection to crush out the weaker ones. Moreover there is a considerable portion of the producing class which, so far from being assisted by production, is systematically handicapped by it. In particular, those domestic producers who are producing for the export market are heavily handicapped not only through the rise of wages and of the costs of production in general, which is the result of any system of protection, but also by the retaliation from abroad which such a system so often provokes. Proceeding further, Schüller remraks that very often, in our times, protection has been so employed as to reduce the purchasing capacity of the consumers with the further result that the domestic producers are injured as a general body. In such cases, "the total result of protection amounts to this, that nobody is permanently benefited while an injury has been inflicted on the population of the entire country".*

Coming to study the actual tariff systems of our times, Schüller has nothing but condemnation for the exaggerated protectionism which inspires them. Many pages are devoted to detailed criticism, but it might be permissible to quote a paragraph summarising the treatment. "Recently Germany has erected a tariff which in its protectionist exaggeration vies with those of the United States, France and Russia. Austria has followed the example of Germany but has preserved greater moderation. Switzerland has enacted a tariff with increased rates, and Russia continues to raise still further its duties which

*Schüller, *Schutzzoll und Freihandel*, pp. 273—280.

are already exorbitant. Even the Balkan States are equipping themselves with prohibitive tariffs. As the result of such a policy, a great proportion of producers is injured, *viz.*, those producing for exportation. But the largest share of the injury is suffered by great masses of operatives through the fall in real wages. Not only is the prevailing type of fiscal policy mischievous from the point of view of the nation as a whole, but it is in the way of ideas of social reform which must form the true bases of the economic and financial systems, of military defence and of culture in general. We must substitute for such a mischievous type of fiscal policy, a policy of rational organization of foreign trade which should be regulated by the interests of a nation as a whole as regards the adjustment of customs duties."*

Schüller has some remarks on the subject of protection to manufactures in the case of a predominantly agricultural country, which deserve attention on account of their application to our local conditions. While agreeing that well-selected duties might be advisably employed in the interests of industrial development, he adds that in the case of such a country, the free importation of a great variety of manufactured articles is beneficial. The result of heavy or general tariffs, in the case of such a country, would be a great rise in the cost of living together with a small growth of industries. Moreover, as an exporter of agricultural produce such a country would be handicapped by the adoption of that policy. According to Schüller, agricultural countries are in a position to derive great advantages from the employment of moderate protectionist duties. The reason assigned is that with the growth of local manufactures in them, the exports of raw materials are automatically reduced, and, as a consequence, the imports of manufactured goods are also automatically reduced without any

---

*Schüller *op. cit.* p. 273.

necessity of piling up heavy duties. On these grounds, Schüller suggests that a policy of moderate protection might well benefit a predominantly agricultural country, while anything like heavy or general protection will injure such a country.*

---

*Schüller, pp. 278—280.

LECTURE IV.

THE INFLUENCE OF PROTECTION ON INDIAN AGRICULTURE, LABOUR AND TRADE.

General effects of the introduction of protection on the distribution of wealth.

In this lecture an attempt will be made to trace and discuss the possible effects of the introduction of industrial protection on the position of agriculture, labour and foreign trade of India. It is well-known that any important change of fiscal policy affects the internal distribution of wealth in a country—whether the change is from proctection to free-trade or from free-trade to protection. In these matters an abundant amount of experience has been acquired as a result of the tariff experiments of the world, mainly during the last century; and, that experience has been garnered for us in the writings both of tariff historians and economists. Indeed, tariff history would have been written in vain, so far as we are concerned, if we did not utilise that material. We shall begin our study with a few generalisations regarding the effects of protection upon the internal distribution of wealth. The effects are different according as we have a case of agrarian protection granted by a predominantly industrial country, or a case of protection to manufactures extended by a predominantly agricultural country. Obviously the latter case is the one which will interest us most in India.

The first case—that of a manufacturing country introducing agrarian protection—need not detain us long. Here the main advantage of the protection is naturally secured for the landlords and the agriculturists, who benefit both by the rise of the prices of agricultural produce as well as by the extension of cultivation and the fall of the margin of cultivation. The burden of protection is shouldered by the consumers in general, but also by wage-earners and manufacturers. The manufacturers will find to their cost, that on account of the rise in the cost of living higher wages are being demanded from them. At the same time they have no additional resource out of which to pay these higher wages. The burden is therefore divided between the manufacturer and the wage-earner. The wages must be raised to a certain extent and thus profits decline, the marginal manufacturers suffering most. But, even so, wages cannot be increased in exact proportion to the rise in the cost of living and consequently the wage earners too have to shoulder a part of burden. Hence the justification of the proposition that agrarian protection is even more unfavourable in its effects on distribution than protection to manufactures.

The effect on distribution is of a different character, when a predominantly agricultural country gives protection to manufactures. In this case too the consumer is hit by the higher cost of living due to the rise in price of the imports as well as of the local substitutes. The nominal wages of labour will tend to rise, but the real wages considered in terms of commodities might easily be reduced if we consider the whole body of labour in the country, and not merely that portion which is employed on good wages in the protected industries. Agricultural production will be hampered by the rise in cost of living, and the higher nominal wages which increase the cost of production. Finally, the agriculturist will be unfavourably affected in his capacity of a purchaser of the manufactured goods—whether foreign or home-made. "In order to secure the same quantity of manufectured articles the agriculturist will have to part with a larger quantity of his own produce."*

We shall now consider how the fortunes of the Indian

---

*For a more detailed analysis on those lines consult the seventh chapter of Fontana-Russo's work on Commercial Policy.

agriculturist would be affected by the introduction of protection. The Commission has noted that so far as protection advances industrial development and increases the wage fund going to the employees in industrial areas, the surrounding rural areas will also benefit, since a portion of these wages will be forwarded to their families residing in the villages. This is, so far as it goes, unquestionably an advantageous thing for agriculture. Conceivably, agriculture might benefit in other ways from any successful industrial development brought about by protection. Only, it has to be understood that such resultant advantages as agriculture can gain from protection will not accure in the immediate future, but will follow after the period required for industrial development ; whereas the less favourable effects of protection on agriculturists, as regards the high cost of living and of production, will follow at once on the inception of protection.

Protection and agriculturist's resources.

It is also possible, that some of the employees in industrial centres might go back to rural occupations with capital saved out of their industrial wages, as also with improved ideas as regards the use of machinery and general organisation of business. So far as any movement in this direction takes place, Indian agriculture will be a gainer. It has further been suggested that with the growth of possibilities of employment in industrial centres, agricultural wages will become more responsive to changes in cost of living. There might be something in this idea, but so far agricultural wages have shown a capacity for increasing *pari passu* with general prices without any extrinsic assistance in the shape of tariff. Dr. Mann's researches show a satisfactory increase in agricultural wages relatively to the cost of living. The Prices Report also tells us that "in rural areas, wages, both of agricultural labourers and village artisans, have risen enormously as measured by the purchasing power of commodities . . . . The rise in the wages of industrial labour has not been as large as in the case of labourers just mentioned." Nevertheless, it is arguable that with the growth in the number of agricultural labourers which is the normal feature as shown by one census after another, it is to some extent useful to possess potentialities of well-paid occupations outside the limits of agriculture.

Protection and the pressure of population on land.

Protection has also been advocated with the object of reducing the pressure on land. It would be preferable to say that the effect of industrial development would be in the direction of some slackening of the increase of such pressure in the future. As the Hon'ble Mr. Harkishen Lall put it before the Fiscal Commission: "It is impossible to conceive that at any stage of India's industrial growth all or half, or even one-third of the agricultural population will be transferred into an industrial population. The numbers are so great in agriculture, and the number required for industries would be so small compared to the population that I cannot conceive a stage when agriculture would be affected by industrial growth." Other witnesses told the same tale. Prof. Jevons argued that "the growth of industries will be slow, and the growth in the town population will be comparatively slow." The authors of these remarks had a true perspective of the proportionate potentialities of the growth of industry and of agriculture in India. Nor need this seemingly slow increase of industrial population disappoint any enthusiast for industrial development; for the argument cuts both ways. If the slow growth of industries cannot do much to reduce the pressure of population on land on the one hand, the same state of things on the other hand relieves us of the fear that industrial development will draw away a considerable proportion of labour from agriculture and would cause an inconvenient reduction of the food supply. Indeed, there are reasons why we should not, if we could, induce a great rural exodus in India. Prof. Basu has emphasised the fact that "industrialisation in the sense of the west need not be too rapid in India, for the mass of the rural population to be able to adapt themselves to the new condition. . . . . The growth of industrial habits among the labouring population is not only a matter of training but also one of temperamental adaptation. This is partly a socio-psychological factor which should not be lost sight of in our passion for developing Indian industries quickly and at any cost." But, really there is no danger of any considerable rural exodus, following on protection. The growth of factory industry has a tendency to deprive a large number of hand workers of their hereditary occupations and many of these men will betake themselves to agriculture. Thus, to take an example, the increase of our cotton mills and of the factory hands employed in them has involved the displacement of a larger number of handworkers (weavers) and many of them have taken to the plough as their principal means of subsistence. Owing to the action of this cause, in the earlier stages of the industrial development of India, there will be two streams of movement of labour—one from agriculture to the new machine-industries and the other from the old hand industries towards agriculture. The problem is thus a highly complicated one.

We must now consider the opinion that protection will produce an increased demand from industrial centres for food products and raw materials, and will in this way benefit the agriculturist. It has to be admitted that such advantage can be expected to accrue, in any substantial measure, only after much time has elapsed and an advanced stage of industrial development has been reached. In anything like the near future not much is to be expected in this direction; we have only to imagine our industrial population of two millions increased even at the great rate of 10 per cent. to get at the annual increase of potential demand, and on the other hand to consider the far greater normal increase of numerous millions of the agricultural population. Looking much further ahead, however, the increased demand from our industrial centres might have tangible effects, especially as the consumption per capita of the industrial operative with his higher wages and standard of living is larger than that of the rural population.

Since the days of the Famine Commission of 1880 the opinion has been advanced that diversity of occupations is the remedy for famines. This, however, is an extreme view. This can be seen easily if it is borne in mind that the main portion of the demand for local manufactures must come from the resources of agricultural produce. So far as these resources are diminished by a famine, the demand for manufactured goods will fall and will diminish the employment in industrial centres except so far as manufactured articles are produced for stock or for export. Indeed, one can go further and show that any particular percentage reduction of agricultural production must diminish the country's demand for manufactures by an even larger percentage. The reason is that as the price of foodstuffs rises, an abnormally large proportion of the incomes of the common people must be spent on food, and hence an unusually small percentage remains to be spent on manufactures. Let us illustrate this by an arithmetical example. Suppose a famine reduces the total agricultural production of India about 20 per cent.; then, obviously, the Indian demand for manufactures must fall at least by that percentage. But that is not all. Suppose, further, that the average agriculturist had been spending in normal years 25 per cent. of his income on manufactures; then in the famine year he must spend less in this direction—say, 15 per cent. The result is that the total purchasing power of the country is reduced on account of the famine, and of this smaller purchasing power a larger proportion than usual is diverted to foodstuffs.

Industrial development as a remedy for famines.

However, though protection cannot afford a direct remedy or mitigation of famines, yet, in the normal years, it might increase the means at the disposal of the agriculturist and consequently his power of resistance against famines when they come. As we have seen above, the industrial wage-earner sends his savings to his native village, and this contribution, if duly saved, increases the resources on which agriculturist can fall back in times of famine. Again, industrial development increases the wealth in urban centres, and co-operative banking might draw on some of it in order to assist the cause of agricultural progress in general.

Possible adverse effects of manufacturing protection on agriculture.

Coming to the adverse effects of protectionism on agriculture, we must concentrate on the one real danger—the increase in the cost of living as well as in the cost of agricultural production; there can be no denying the reality of this drawback of a protectionist policy. A rise in the cost of living due to protection must raise wages in agrarian areas and, consequently, the cost of production to the agriculturist. Further, any protectionist duty which raises the price of materials or implements (*e.g.*, machinery) used by the agriculturist contributes to the rise of the cost of production to his detriment. To these considerations a rejoinder has been attempted, to the effect that, because our rural population does not consume a large proportion of imported articles it will be unaffected by the rise in their prices due to protection. But, those who urge this view are neglecting an important factor in the situation; a rise in the price of imported goods is almost always accompanied by an increase in the price of their locally produced substitutes. Thus, it may be true, that the humble agrarian does not consume much of the imported sugar; but if a protective duty is imposed on foreign sugar the first effect will be the rise in the price of *gur*. This is a well established position of theory, and has also been backed up by the opinion of experts on the practical side. Thus, as a producer, the landowner will be in a less favourable position after the advent of protection; and the same might be said of him in his capacity of a consumer of manufactures. In a protectionist regime "manufacturers find themselves in a privileged position, since in order to procure the same amount of manufactured articles, the agriculturist will have to surrender a larger quantity of agricultural products.* He can in the main benefit only so far as he produces less food crops and more of the commercial crops—raw materials demanded by the new manufactures.

It is true, that during the period which extended over the twenty years 1891—1911, the cost of living rose considerably in India and yet the Indian cultivator was no worse off than before. During that period, the income of the agricultural classes rose as fast as, if not faster than, the general level of prices; but it has to be noted that the chief factor in the rise of cost of living during that period was the increase in the prices of the products of agriculturists; only a comparatively small share of the result was due to the rise in the prices of manufactured articles. On the other hand in the protectionist era, which we are envisaging, the increase in the cost of living will be due entirely to the rise in the price of manufactured articles. The change in price levels will not present any feature favourable to the agriculturist. There are some further ways also to be considered in which protection might possibly affect the prosperity of the landowner adversely. Thus, in some predominantly agricultural countries there have been complaints that protection has been the indirect cause of the reduction of agricultural exports, the national imports are checked by protectionist duties, and this fall of imports is followed by a reduction of exports and among others generally, agricultural exports have been reduced. Thus during the debates on the French Tariff of 1910, M. Jaures showed that there was a great possibility of increasing the exports of agricultural products from France; but that this potentiality could be realised only on the condition that the tariff barriers against international trade were lowered. French viticulture, in particular, desired foreign markets; but

---

*Fontana-Russo *op. cit.*, p. 323.

these markets could not be opened until the French tariffs were lowered. So also in Italy protection has been accused of preventing a due expansion of the exports of the fruits of the soil in exchange for foreign manufactures. The agrarian in that country has learnt from personal experience that in order to sell, he must buy.* In view of the fact that a large proportion of India's exports are of an agricultural character the experience of other countries provides a strong argument against the introduction of high or indiscriminate protection.

It has been alleged, that industrial development under protection might cause a scarcity of labour for agricultural operations. Apprehensions of this character were expressed by the Madras Ryotwari Landholders' Association before the commission. They express the view that "industries should be located in such places that the population will not be drawn away to towns." They admitted that our agricultural labourers are not fully employed, but urged that agricultural operations could not dispense with the present available population in the rural tracts. "We require the services of the agriculturists, say, during five months in the year; we cannot distribute the same work throughout the year so as to dispense with a certain amount of the population. The whole village population will be required during these five months."

The problem thus propounded is a highly complicated one; in the first place regard must be had to the fact that here is a seasonal demand for a great proportion of the existing rural population and thus it is not possible to spare a very large proportion of it for the task of industrial development, unless there is a great improvement in agricultural methods and organisation. On the other hand, we have to consider the very great normal increase in the rural population of India which is so considerable as to remove all fears of any *general* shortage of

*On this topic the student would do well to consult Aug. Arnauné: *Le Commerce exterieur et les Tarifs de Douane* (pp. 343-344) as well as Augier and Marvaud, *La Politique Douaniere de la France* (pp. 55—58).

agricultural labour resulting from industrial development. Nor is the progress of industrial development in India likely to be so precipitate as some enthusiasts would make out. We have already quoted the very sensible and pertinent remark of the Hon'ble Mr. Harkishen Lal:—"the numbers are so great in agriculture and the number required for industries would be so small compared to the population that I cannot conceive a stage when agriculture would be affected by industrial growth." We are very far indeed from the stage attained by the manufacturing nations of the West, where we have an embarassing drain of labour from agriculture towards manufacturing centres. France, indeed, complains of insufficiency of agricultural labour on account of the drain towards industrial centres, and similarly the German landowners are complaining of "Leutenot" or want of agricultural labour. We in India, however, have no reason to anticipate any such general scarcity of labour for the fields; though no doubt in a great number of rural areas adjoining industrial centres the difficulties of the landowner in obtaining labour will be greatly increased. Thus, we are already told how "the small holder, especially in Gujerat, complains that his labourers desert him for the mills and only inferior workers are obtainable. The continuance of these conditions must re-act upon the standard of cultivation which in Gujerat has always been high. Many landholders have been compelled to lease out their lands to men who were formerly their labourers." Similarly in the Central Provinces and Berar "with the increased wages for paid labour there is a marked tendency to restrict the extension of the home-farm." A great deal of such local difficulties regarding agriculture must be expected with industrial development. Indeed, they are somewhat inconsistent who argue that industrial improvement will raise money wages and in the same breath assert that there need not be any fears even of a local shortage of agricultural labour.

The experience of protection in other countries shows how,

under it, the agriculturist has to bear the burden of high costs of living and of production ; and tariff literature abounds in protests raised by the agricultural communities against the protectionist policy. In America the South was always opposed to heavy protection. Nor was the opposition of the agrarian party in America to protection mitigated until either genuine protection, or, at least in some cases, the fiction of protection was secured for agriculture as well. Thus, discussing the American Tariff of 1883 Prof. Taussig points out that under it the duties on a number of agricultural products were left unchanged, and then he goes on to observe that "it is needless to say that the duties on them had no effect whatever, except to an insignificant extent on the local trade across the Canadian border. *The duties were left unchanged in order to maintain the fiction that the agricultural population secured through them a share of the benefits of protection.** Similarly the late Prof. Rabbeno observed that "the agricultural states of the South were in favour of free-trade, the manufacturing ones of the North in favour of protection; a terrible war was the outcome. At present antagonism of this kind still exists to a certain extent, and discontent with the protectionist policy is spreading in the West. But the complaints of the agriculturists have been partly silenced by means of agrarian protection, which is now keeping pace in the United States with that of manufactures." Elsewhere the same authority remarks as follows:—"Now, considering on one hand that a vigorous agricultural protection neutralises the advantages that protection to manufactures can offer to capitalists, and that *in reality the American agriculturists are not in want of this protection, but they have demanded it up to the present time more as a recompense for the industrial protection than for any other reason* ; so that it seems very slightly

Opposition offered by agrarians to manufacturing protection in other countries.

*Taussig, *Tariff History*, p. 249.

probable that they should demand it in preference to the reduction of all tariffs."* These remarks might be suitably supplemented by Dr. Marshall's statement that the protective tariffs of America "hindered the development of the agricultural resources of the country. This involved some retardation of the growth of commercial centres ; which are nearly, though not quite, as important from the social point of view as the industrial centres."* The same eminent writer refers to the argument of the American advocates of protection to manufactures that since the farmers had been allowed to take up the great expanse of rich agricultural land in the country, there was no injustice in compelling them to contribute to the building up of progressive industries. To this the agriculturists could reply that they "had only availed themselves of opportunities for hard, if not hazardous, ventures, which were open to every one ; that no exclusive favour had been granted to them after they had once committed themselves to their tasks ; and that therefore they were not in a similar position to manufacturers who asked for favours."

The opposition of interests between the agricultural South and the manufacturing North was both felicitously and eloquently expressed by McDuffie one of the Southern orators in a speech in 1830. "The great misfortune is, sir,—and it gives us the true key to this whole system—that, while this Government is an undivided and indivisible unity, the country over which it extends is divided into various and—disguise it as we may—diametrically adverse interests. Hence, it results, that the law which throws a restriction upon the commerce of the Southern States, to the great and obvious injury of the planter, is obviously calculated, and professedly intended, to promote the interest of the Northern manufacturer. If the manufacturer can gain 10 per cent. by the restriction, it is his interest to adhere to it, though it imposes a burden of 40 or

*Rabbeno, *American Commercial Policy*, p. 254 and p. 209.
*Marshall,—*Industry and Trade* pp. 763—764.

50 per cent. upon the planter. Hence it is that majority of this House are pursuing a policy with regard to the interests of the whole Union, which no human being would pursue in regard to his own interests."*

In Germany, also, it has been found necessary to increase agricultural protection, because protection to manufactures had been found to be reducing agrarian profits. Thus we read in the preamble to the German Tariff Bill of 1902 as follows:—"A collateral effect of the industrial expansion has been the larger demands made by the agricultural labourers who have withstood the movement to the towns, thus *greatly increasing the working expenses of agriculture, and making that industry in most of its branches less profitable. Hence the necessity for more protection.*"

The opinion has also been expressed by Indian economists that the agriculture of the country will have to pay a good part of the price of industrial development obtained through protection. The expression of such opinions is naturally to be expected on the part of gentlemen representing predominantly agricultural provincess like Madras and the Punjab. Thus Mr. C. Ramalinga Reddy observed before the Fiscal Commission that "in so far as protection could be expected to have any influence, I believe that temporarily at least it will either depress the rural classes still further or render their economical recovery slower and more difficult." He based his view partly on his experience and partly on the constant struggles between agrarians and industrialists in different parts of the world.

Our examination of the possible effects of protection on Indian agriculture leads us to the conclusion that the agriculturist will have to contribute his full share of the sacrifice involved by protection for a considerable length of time; both as producer and as consumer he will be adversely affected and

---

*Callender,—*Economic History of the United States* p. 524.

this constitutes an additional argument for discriminating and moderate protection. Anything like heavy protection will affect the agriculturist adversely, not only as a producer and a consumer, but as one deeply interested in the export trade of India. Among agrarians themselves the largest measure of sacrifice must come from the landowner. The agricultural wage earner will generally have to see his cost of living rise perceptibly ; on the other hand the agricultural operative in the rural areas adjoining industrial districts will certainly benefit. It is unfortunately not possible in India to compensate the agriculturist directly by introducing agrarian protection *pari passu* with protection to manufacturing industries, as has been done in other countries. There, indeed, "the adhesion to the protectionist policy on the part of the agricultural regions was obtained by extending the benefits of the system in generous measure to the products of the soil."* We are in no condition to introduce protection at once to manufacture and to agriculture. Consequently, for any general improvement of the conditions of all ranks of agriculturists we shall have to wait for a considerable time, and for a great and successful progress of industrial development.

Money wages in protected industries.

In proceeding to study the possible effects of protection on the wage-earner we have to consider separately the prospects of the industrial labourer in the protected and unprotected industries, as well as those of unskilled and agricultural labour. It is certain, that the money wages of skilled labour in the protected industries will experience a considerable and immediate rise. The aggregate supply of skilled labour in the country is, relatively speaking, small and inelastic, and this fact is favourable to the rise of wages in this particular case. It is however, only as the efficiency of these highly paid operatives increases that their wages will cease to be reflected in high costs

*Stanwood, *American Tariff Controversies*, Vol. II, p. 158.

of production and high prices to the consumer. Much will depend upon the attitude which labour assumes when the opportunities of getting high money wages are opened out to it. If labour responds by increasing its efficiency and regularity of work, the country will be the gainer. Thus the inclination of its labourers to do assiduous work in return for fair wages has been a great asset to Germany. On the other hand in Australia there is a tendency for labour and capital to combine to raise protection and to increase profits as well as wages steadily at the expense of the consumer.

Money wages in unprotected industries.

In the unprotected industries, also, there will be a partial tendency towards increase of wages. In fact, as regards wages, the protected industries will set the pace and the unprotected industries will have to follow rather reluctantly. This will raise costs of production in the unprotected industries which will be thus forced to shoulder some share of the burden of protection without being in a position to enjoy the benefits of protection. As regards unskilled industrial labour, this sort of "sympathetic effect" might be expected to cause a slight rise of wages; but this rise will presumably be much smaller than the increase of wages in the case of skilled labour, the reason being that the potential supply of unskilled labour is very large in the case of India.

Effect of protection on real wages.

So far we have spoken about the rise of money wages; it now remains to consider how the real wages in terms of commodities are likely to be affected. It is the general experience of all protectionist countries that the rise of prices neutralises in a great measure the rise of nominal wages. Thus German economists admit freely that the cost of living of labour was higher in protectionist Germany than in England; in other words "with an equal expenditure, an English workman was better fed than a German."* Similarly, in America with its high tariffs, the money wages are much higher than in Europe; but the difference in real wages is not so great. In our country too, the rise of real wages will be smaller than that of money wages; and here again the skilled operative of protected industries will be in a somewhat privileged position. There is indeed, one factor which in some protectionist countries benefits the industrial operator in the matter of real wages, but at the expense of the agriculturist. It might happen that the diminution of manufacturing imports might in turn cause of reductiou of agricultural exports. This result, if it is reached, lowers the price of food grain temporarily, and thus relieves the industrial operative to some extent of the burden of a rising cost of living.* Needless to say however that such a result is far from being desirable.

In the interest both of industrial and agricultural labour a moderate scale of duties is to be desired, since high duties would greatly raise the cost of living to our labouring classes by increasing the prices both of imported commodities and of the locally produced substitutes. Moreover, it is only in certain favourably situated districts that protection can be expected to raise even the money wages of the agrarian; such are the rural districts adjoining industrial centres, or those which for some local reason are already suffering from a paucity of agricultural labour.

Effect of protection on cost of living.

Proceeding to consider the effects of a protectionist policy on the interests of the national consumer, it needs to be emphasised that all protectionist countries have comparatively high price levels and high costs of living. This result is brought about by the cumulative action of protection at once upon prices and upon costs

*Clapham, *Economic Development of France and Germany*, p. 406, and Schmoller, *op. cit.* Vol. II. p. 298.

*Cf. Fontana-Russo, *op. cit.* p. 322.

of production. The protectionist duty raises the domestic price of the protected article as well as the cost of production of other articles in the manufacture of which the former article figures as a raw material. There is another way in which protection makes for high level of prices—*viz.*, by tending to restrict imports. As Dr. Marshall has felicitously put it, "the purchasing power of money in any country may be affected by its tariff policy, for taxes on certain imports into a country raise their value in that country relatively to things which are not taxed; and one of them is gold. Therefore the purchasing power of gold is generally low in a country which levies many high import duties."*

Abundant authority could be brought forward to testify to the undoubted fact that prices and cost of living are high in countries with a high protective tariff. Dr. Marshall himself verified the statement that in "the comparatively free-trade period of Germany the purchasing power of money was two-thirds as high again in Germany as in England". In more recent times the high tariffs in that country "have so raised prices against the consumer, that the real wages of the German workman have risen less rapidly than those of the English." Professor Brentano might be quoted as another author who has written much to show that "as the result of protection all prices, especially the prices of rural and urban land, have risen to an extraordinary degree in Germany. The cost of living has been rising pretty continuously with the increased tariffs." Schmoller also says that although the prices of grain and foodstuffs hardly rose with the duties until 1887, they did increase later, though not by the full amount of the duties.

The great protectionist authorities are very far from denying that one effect of protection must be to increase prices. List.

---

*Cf. Marshall, *Money, Credit and Commerce*, pp. 198—200; also, the same author's *Fiscal Policy of International Trade* s. 3 and s. 20.

himself has argued in many cases that as the result of protection prices must rise, to start with, and manufacturers will make extraordinary profits ; "but the consumers have ample security that these extra-ordinary profits shall not reach unreasonable limits, or become perpetual, by means of the competition at home which follows later on".* Admitting the truth of the general idea propounded by List, it must be said that he greatly underestimated the length of the infancy and the developmental period of industries. More recent theorists on the protectionist side like Grunzel, with a greater experience of the results of tariff policies, admit fully that economic protectionism must increase price levels. Grunzel indeed argues that "the general level of prices may be driven by a protective policy to extraordinary heights when the economic conditions permit of its working out its full effect." The same author argues further that the effect of the protective policy is not limited to the prices of the dutiable imports: it also influences the prices of cheaper local substitutes by diverting demand to them and in this fact he finds the rationale of excise duties. He further urges that protective policy might easily affect the prices of commodities in general in unexpected ways. All consumption goods stand in a competitive relation as regards the consumer and if, as the result of protection, the consumer has to expend more of his income on the protected goods he must spend less on other commodities.*

The effect of protectionist import duties on the domestic price of dutiable articles might be here considered very briefly. It might be said that the deciding factors in this matter are in the first place, the nature of the demand for import and the comparative elasticity or extensibility of the supply of the particular commodity in the exporting and importing countries respectively. If the demand of the importing country for the

---

*List, *op. cit.*, p. 137.

*Grunzel, *Economic Protectionism*, pp. 309—310.

article in question is urgent or inelastic, the protectionist duty will raise the price considerably. A practical corollary of this proposition is that great caution should be used in imposing protectionist import duties on the necessaries of life. In the second place, we have to consider the expansibility or elasticity of the local supply so far as the local production is susceptible of extension, and, if sufficient capital and other resources for extending it are at hand, the rise in the domestic price due to the protectionist duty is comparatively smaller. On the other hand, should the local supply of the commodity have little expansibility or elasticity, the consumer will be heavily burdened by the duty without much advantage accuring to the industrialist. The practical corollary from this reasoning is that protection should be applied with discrimination, and generally speaking, only to such industries as possess the requisite condition for rapid expansion—*i.e.*, to industries with a high degree of elasticity of supply.

As might be expected, there is a close connection between the rate of the protectionist duties levied and the rise in the domestic prices of the dutiable goods. Prof. Taussig has developed this aspect of import duties, following some earlier suggestions made by the distinguished American publicist, Gallatin. He first considers the case in which an import duty is levied exactly equal to the difference between the local and the foreign cost of production. Here if, after the imposition of the duty, imports continue to come over the tariff barrier in substantial quantities and for a fairly long period, it might be assumed with justice, that the local price of the commodities has risen by the full amount of the duty. Not only is the price of the foreign imports raised by the full amount but also that of the similar local products. Obviously, in this case Prof. Taussig assumes that the elasticity of the domestic supply is not very great. The same author considers another case in which the import duty is greater than the difference between the local and foreign cost; in this case the price will generally not rise by the entire amount of the import duty.*

It is such considerations combined with a due regard to the poverty of the Indian masses that naturally inclines a great many economists in India to a policy of moderate duties. Thus, Prof. Basu emphasises the fact that the average income in Germany and America is more than ten times the average income of an Indian. "Therefore what the former can afford to spend for the luxury of a political experiment like protection is required by the latter to keep the wolf from the door." So also Prof. K. T. Shah of the Bombay University has argued that "the strongest plea of Free-Trade in India is that of cheapness; given the almost incredible poverty of the Indian people, the policy which claims cheapness to the consumer as the guiding maxim cannot but command a most respectful attention.........It is certain that in the next generation the popular party in India, assuming India to become a self-governing democracy, will have to reckon with this argument." For over two decades a continuous rise of prices has been pressing on the modest means of the Indian consumer. Protection and the resultant industrial development will, let us hope, increase the average income in India after some more decades, but during the period of transition, anything more than a very moderate protection will tax the slender resources of the Indian purchaser. Hence the repeated demand before the Fiscal Commission for a "judicious, gradual and moderate protection." It was an industrial representative of Bombay who asserted before the Fiscal Commission that "India is a poor country, and I am not in favour of high tariffs which a rich country like America can indulge in with impunity."

---

*Taussig, *Aspects of the Tariff Question*, chapter I; and *cf.* Gallatin's Memorial in *State papers and speeches on the Tariff.*

Among consumers taken as a body, there is one class with a fairly high traditional standard of living which has derived little advantage from the economic changes of the last twenty or thirty years. A series of investigations, both official and private, have familiarised us with the fact that the middle classes have been hard hit by the continuous rise of prices, and have consequently failed to show any signs of marked improvement in their economic condition. They have inherited the doubtful blessing of a traditional and comparatively high standard of living which includes the use of a considerable number of imported articles, and they have striven with fair success to keep up the standard. The latest witness to their declining fortunes was the Committee on Indian Exchange and Currency. The process of the adjustment of wages to a rising level of prices has been slow enough, but the middle class is still awaiting the indefinite process of any adjustment of its income. There is no doubt that this class will be the greatest sufferer with any rise of prices due to protection.

Influence of protection on the economic condition of our middle class.

Nor is a member of this class in any position to turn to very good account such opportunities for employment as the protectionist regime is likely to offer. In the competition for the new directive and supervising jobs he has formidable rivals among the class of skilled artisans who possess those hereditary instincts for taking a prominent part in industrial transactions which heredity has denied to him ; consequently his will be in the main the clerical task, as usual. His rising expenses have drained him of his scanty means and, thus, he cannot benefit in any material degree by the new possibilities of investment which an industrial development under the auspices of protection might open up.

A clearer perception of the nature, extent and duration

of the burden imposed on the consumer by protectionist measures can be attained by a consideration of statistical studies of prices in countries like America. That country might be regarded as the world's laboratory for tariff experiments, and Prof. Taussig, formerly the President of the American Tariff Commission, has published a number of such enlightening studies. He asserts with justification that in the case of the American iron industry the object of protection to young industries seems to have been attained. He then proceeds to calculate the sacrifice which had to be made in order to attain this success. He finds that for twenty-five years after the beginning of the manufacture in America the local price ranged higher than the British as a result of the duty. "During many of the years between 1870 and 1895 imports of steel rails were considerable, showing that the domestic price was higher than the foreign price by the full amount of the duty. During other years of this period imports ceased ; but domestic prices, though not higher by the full amount of the duty, were still considerably higher. Throughout the quarter century the protective duty raised the price of total supply whether imported or domestic." It must be noted that this was a specially favourable case of the application of protection to a nascent industry. The resources of raw material for the industry at the disposal of America are unique ; so are the resources of capital, business leadership and mechanical ingenuity. It was eminently a case of an industry in which the Law of Increasing Return was fully applicable, and it can be argued that wherever this law applies, the rise of price due to a protective tax is particularly small. Nevertheless, we find that in spite of all these favourable circumstances, America had to pay a heavy price for quarter of a century before the acquisition of the industry was completed. In other industries for which the country enjoyed fewer facilities the price to be paid was pro-

Statistics of the influence of protection on prices.

portionately greater. Thus, as regards the protective duty on sugar "we could say with confidence that from 1897 to 1913 the price of sugar was raised, the country over, by the full amount of the duty." Again as regards the protective duty on wool, "the conclusion would seem warranted that the whole supply, domestic as well as foreign, was raised in price by the full amount of the duty." We thus come to see that while America succeeded in several instances in helping its infant industries forward by the instrumentality of protection, she had a stiff price to pay, in spite of the unusually great productive resources at her disposal.

Effect of protection on the export and import trade.

The analysis of the effects of protection on the trade of India has been carried out by the Fiscal Commission; but it might be a little further developed here. Taking the import trade to start with, we might study the influence of protection upon it, and this is best done by classifying the series of effects according to the periods of time under consideration. It has been emphasised before this, that in the field of fiscal policy the mixing up of long period and short period effects is a common source of fallacies. When we look to the effects of protection upon our import trade in the immediate future, we have to bear in mind that there are two influences of opposite and conflicting character to be taken into account. In the first place, the imposition of protectionist duty must restrict imports to a certain extent—the more so, as the middle class which consumes them so largely at present will feel the strain of the rise in cost of living consequent upon the introduction of protection. On the other hand, we shall have a force working in the opposite direction and tending to increase the volume of imports; a great deal of machinery and technical apparatus will be imported for the use of the industries started under the protectionist regime. It has been noted that when protection was introduced into Russia the import trade consisted predominantly of the necessary materials and machinery for the new industrial concerns that had been started.* In the course of perhaps a few decades this stream of imports in general will begin to slacken. If we care to look further decades ahead, and to assume that industrial development has been rapidly, widely and successfully pushed forward, we might find the volume of imports increasing as the result of a prosperity based upon the maturity of our manufactures. Attention might be drawn here to a potential increase of another item of our imports as a consequence of the introduction of protection. If a wise policy is followed as regards freely admitting foreign capital, our exchanges might be strengthened by the increased flow of such foreign resources in our direction—it being noted that not all the capital moving our way would enter India in the shape of plant, material or equipment of industry.

We might next proceed to examine the influence of protection on our export trade. In the immediate future, our export trade is not like to be affected by the tariff; but, looking a little ahead, we shall find several influences tending towards the diminution of that trade. In the first place, the rise of cost of production and of price levels in the country which would be brought about by protection will tend to reduce our exports. The reduction of imports to start with will mean a favourable balance of trade in the very first stage of the introduction of protection. That means of course a higher price level and a consequent reduction of exports. Another influence also will be acting to reduce our exports. Our foreign customers must buy less of our agricultural and other exports from us when they have been hindered by our tariffs from selling their goods to us as before. Instances can be cited of countries like France which have seen their agricultural exports reduced or become stagnant after they have entered on the paths of protection to industries. It can of course be

---

*Schmoller, *op. cit.*, Vol. II. p. 625.

argued that, after a long period to come, and when the manufacture started under protection have come into maturity, a stimulus might be given to the export trade of India, since the products of the new industries will have begun to be exported. It will however take a long time to reach such a position, because as we have seen the period of the infancy of industries tends to be prolonged with the growth of the scale and the complexity of industry.

It remains to consider the influence of the introduction of protection on the balance of trade of the country. During the first phase supervening on the introduction of protection, the balance of trade tends to be favourable excepting so far as the imports of machinery and technical apparatus will increase largely. If a longer period is considered we shall find both our imports and exports being reduced ; though we have the satisfaction of knowing that the inelastic nature of the demand for some of our exports will counteract this tendency to some extent as regards our exports. Some reduction of our trade both on the import and export side might thus be anticipated as one of the effects of protection. It has also been argued that protection is likely to affect not only size of our balance of trade but its stability. The reduction of exports and imports implies the diminution of the items of trade on both sides; consequently, as has been pointed out, any disturbing factor is more likely to tell on the balance of trade. In manipulating our fiscal policy our tariff-makers will have to foresee and to try minimise the likely effects of protection both on our balance of trade and on its stability.

The opinion that the inauguration of protection is likely to have an unfavourable influence on the total volume of the foreign trade of India was supported by a large number of witnesses who appeared before the Indian Fiscal Commission. So, Prof. Jevons argued that both the exports and imports of India would be smaller but that the development of internal trade would compensate for the loss of foreign trade. The effect of imposing high import duties will at first be to increase the favourable balance of trade by reducing imports. "That will tend to create a higher price level in India and through the operation of that higher price level you will get your exports cut down and you can establish your balance of trade again."

A similar view was propounded by Prof. R. M. Joshi, to the effect that protection was likely to reduce the total volume of India's foreign trade as well as to affect adversely our usually favourable balance of trade. "The large favourable balance of trade which India normally enjoys might be seriously diminished. The working of the gold exchange standard, which depends upon a large favourable balance of trade, might thereby be endangered. But as I have no love for the gold exchange standard, I shall only be happy if circumstances compel the replacement of the gold exchange standard by a strict gold standard." It might be pertinent to ask, however, how we can secure the basis of a strict gold standard in the absence of a favourable balance of trade ; this, however, is a side-issue.

The experience of other protectionist countries might afford some useful guidance for economic anticipations in the case of a protectionist India. Generally speaking unless a country is peculiarly favoured as regards natural resources, and industrial capacity, some slackening of the foreign trade of a country is to be expected for some years after the introduction of protection. Even in the case of Germany the introduction of protection reduced the imports very tangibly for some time, while the German export trade did not make so much progress as was expected by the advocates of protection. Schäffle thus summed up the results of a decade of protection: "The best that can be said is that our foreign trade including that in manufactures, has neither in import nor export stood still, but this fact must not as a matter of course, if at all, be claimed to the credit of the system of high protection. The transit trade and the commission trade in corn, timber, and colonial goods have unquestionably, and in part irremediably, suffered, and with them the railway returns. Industry has on the whole prospered in a gratifying measure but so it did during the fourteen years of free-trade prior to 1879."* It appeared as if Germany "was about to lose a great part of her tolerably stable export trade." These well-grounded fears were set at rest by a series of commercial treaties inaugurated by Count Von Caprivi. Schmoller calls these treaties and the resultant lowering of protectionist barriers "an act of salvation" for the export trade of Germany. The author of these treaties vindicated them by asserting that the lowering of protectionist duties was necessary if the export trade of Germany was to improve, "It is not" he argued "a question of Free-Trade or Protection. These are dogmas and the battle-cry of parties, which do not apply to the situation...... It was necessary by means of customs treaties to extend Germany's markets abroad for her exports.........Germany must either export wares or men." Thus the experience of the first decade of protection in the case of Germany was that protection, unless it is moderate and judicious, handicaps the growth of foreign trade. "The true verdict upon the tariffs of 1879, 1885, and 1887 is contained in the simple fact that the welfare of German industry required in 1892 that the protective barriers should be lowered."

The policy of high protection affected adversely the foreign trade of France for several decades; economic historians whether of the free-trade or of the protectionist school agree in attributing the comparative stagnation of the French export trade to the influence of a heavy tariff. Nobody will accuse Schmoller of any animus against protection. He sums up the situation in France by saying that "protection has not destroyed the foreign trade of France, but it has certainly not helped it.

---

*Cf. Dawson, *Protection in Germany* p. 105 and Schmoller *op. cit.* Vol. II. p. 635.

forward," the imports and exports of manufactures remain almost stable during the protectionist epoch, 1892—1901, as compared with the preceding free-trade decade. French manufactures remained stagnant in the same epoch and then shared only to a small extent in the world-wide progress. Another authority on the same subject, Prof. Meredith asserts that "the return to protection in France coincided with a marked slackening in the expansion of that country's foreign trade and that this relative decline became more marked as the country plunged more deeply into protection." For the most recent study on the subject we are indebted to Dr. J. H. Clapham. He shows that France was successful in her object of becoming almost self-supporting—at a price. "The price was paid in many ways. Part of it in rather stagnant exports; for the nation that will not buy, neither shall it sell".*

To trace the possible effects of protection on the foreign trade of a country is one of the most complicated tasks to which an economist can address himself. It is fortunate therefore, that we have the advantage of being able to refer to Schmoller's brilliant review of the progress of the foreign trade of European countries under the protectionist regime. His general view is that "naturally all free-trade policies afford a stimulus to the increase of foreign trade, while all protectionist policies have the opposite tendency." But he emphasises the view that foreign trade depends in its nature upon a number of causes of which fiscal policy is by no means the most important. In his opinion, protection has not been able to reduce the foreign trade of Germany because that country is under the necessity of importing both food and raw material and because it must export manufactures as well as capital. Russia and Austria have increased their foreign commerce in spite of protection, because they had great powers of agricultural export. Nor is the relatively stationary condition of the foreign trade of France

*Clapham *op. cit.* p. 183.

due exclusively to her protectionist policy. On similar grounds we have argued that the view so often strongly expressed as regards the adverse influence of protection on the volume of the foreign trade of India has much to justify it ; and that heavy tariffs would certainly reduce both the foreign trade of the country and the amount as well as the stability of our usually favourable balance of trade.

LECTURE V.

SOME INFANT INDUSTRIES OF INDIA.

The paper-making industry, its present stage of transition.

Without usurping the functions of the Tariff Board, in the slightest measure, we might illustrate the application of the Infant Industry argument from existing Indian industries. By selecting a few types of such industries and by discussing the circumstances relating to them, it can be shown what considerations strengthen or weaken the case for the application of protection to young industries. No attempt can be made, in such a brief study, to be exhaustive either as regards the industries dealt with, or in the matter of working out the various aspects of each industry which are of interest to the student of the fiscal policy. It requires a detailed study of each industry to decide on the rate of protection to be extended to it. What follows consists only of illustrations of the types of nascent industries in India and of the general considerations to be utilised in making out a *prima facie* case for the extension or refusal of tariff help to such industries.

The first type we shall examine is represented by the paper-making industry. Besides the consideration due to the fact that it is a young industry, it is further to be emphasised, that it is now entering on a transition period, in resorting to the permanent and abundant supply of bamboo-pulp which will help it ultimately to a much cheaper and larger source of raw material than its available to its foreign rivals. As the distinguished Forest Economist Mr. R. S. Pearson told the Fiscal Commission, the cost of making bamboo-pulp would be Rs. 1.9 per maund, and that of making it from sabai grass is Rs. 2.8 per maund, while that the imported sulphide spruce is Rs. 2.75 per maund. At present there are only three bamboo-mills in India; but if time was afforded to develop the new resource available in the shape of bamboo-pulp, the Indian paper-mills can not only held their own against foreign competion but can ultimately command a large export trade. There is another consideration in favour of giving special assistance which should not be lost sight of. Bamboo-pulp has a great advantage over wood-pulp, in the fact that the growth of trees for wood-pulp is slow, and it takes thirty or forty years to replace the trees which have been cut down; whereas bamboos can be reproduced almost every year. Experiments carried on in Burma show that "with a four-year cropping, the bamboo in no way deteriorates. At the end of ten years there are more bamboos on the area than there were when they started cutting." On the other hand a paper factory using wood-pulp can be said to be "living on its capital from the start", and is in need of a constant re-afforesting policy. Mr. Raitt, a high expert on the matter, has analysed the subject from the point of view of comparative cost of production, and he considers that "there is every prospect of Indian-made bamboo-pulp competing with the imported pulp, not only in India but in other Eastern markets".

Large sums of money have been spent in valuable experiments with bamboo-pulp in India. But the experiments have been interrupted by dumping of temporarily cheaper pulp from abroad. Protection is necessary only for a short period to set the mills in a permanently advantageous position as regards foreign competition. To say this is not to deny that great improvements are necessary in the organisation, equipment and scale of our paper-mills. But no doubt our paper and paper-pulp industry, seems to afford an unusually favourable field for the application of the infant industries argument.

It remains to explain why we regard paper-making and pulp-manufacture as a special type among the infant industries of India. It is because it is entering on a period industrial transition and change of process; and economists of authority are, as we have seen, of opinion that any period of transition and of great industrial change offers special advantageous opportunities for extending protection to infant industry. In the case of the paper industry in India there is, to all appearance warrant for applying this dictum and for putting into practice the implied recommendation.

Its remarkable progress.

It is true that several years ago, Prof. Lees Smith condemned our paper-mills for their unprogressive methods and for their not having developed adequately in spite of the protection which they already enjoyed in the shape of government support and custom. Since that time, however, the Indian paper-mills have made a very creditable record during the war and might be said to have completely retrieved their position. "By the aid of the Indian Mills, the armies in India, in Mesopotamia and to some extent Egypt have been kept supplied with paper and forms; the wants of the civil administration in India and in some of the further East colonies have been met, and though the private purchaser in this country had had his difficulty, all essential publications have been maintained without break." The Indian mills have been accused of making large profits, "but it must be remembered that most of the ordinary sorts of paper in England have cost consumers from half as much again to double the price at which they have been procurable in India." Again during the war the Indian Paper Mills have undertaken the manufacture of special kinds of paper which had been formerly imported. Finally their higher profits during the war has furnished them with resources for materially improving their equipment.*

But, although, we see an undoubtedly strong case both for transport and other concessions as well as for tariff help, we also meet with some of those practical difficulties which prove so perplexing both to the student of economics and even more to the conscientious legislator. The publishing trade is full of

*Cf. *Indian Munition Board's Hand-book,* pp. 252—253.

apprehensions as regards the possibilties of tariff help to the paper-making industry. It is pointed out that printed books are admitted, and indeed must be admitted, into the country free of duty, while at the same time the local production of books would be handicapped if the price of paper rose as the result of protection to the paper industry. Apart from the interest of the publishing trade the claims of public intelligence and education cannot be safely or rightly ignored. This undoubtedly great conflict of interests strengthens our conclusion that only a moderate protection should be added to any other concessions claimed by the paper industry.

The factors affecting the claim of the Indian paper industry to protection might be recapitulated. That industry deserves well of the country in that it has not been content to follow the old and conservative methods, but has made a serious effort to avail itself of the promising and novel source of raw material which our country can supply. The result of this is, in the opinion of experts, a certain and considerable reduction in the cost of production of the Indian article below that of its rivals. The possession of such a unique raw material is in itself a great comparative advantage for the local industry. Even apart from that new development, the industry has been making good its position. As Mr. Barbour observes in a recent article on this subject, India was at a disadvantage in the matter of the utilization of wood-pulp. "Wood-pulp has proved the dire enemy of the Indian paper maker. Yet he himself makes use of it as it combines to advantage with grass fibres in paper. He can with its aid speed up production and by increased outturn diminish his general overhead costs per ton of paper made. He has thus as it were, drawn strength from his enemy."* He has also, it might be added made a creditable attempt to bring into existence subsidiary and parallel industries like the opening up of the deposits of Kaolin and the manufacture of caustic soda

*_Journal of Indian Industries and Labour_, Nov. 1921, p. 449.

and bleach. The local industry while making this progress has been exposed to a long course of dumping from foreign countries, nor does the future bear the promise of any mitigation in this respect. Consequently, the industry can show a *prima facie* case for protection. At the same time, it has to be said that import duties are not the only, nor even the most important, kind of assistance that the industry stands in need of. It has also demanded "an improvement in the provision of railway transport and favourable treatment in regard to railway rates"—a claim which requires careful investigation. Nor, of course, can any such assistance absolve the paper industry from making further needful efforts to lower its cost of production. Thus, the Canadian Trade Commissioner has pointed out that in India "the four largest mills produce only 96 tons per day between them and the largest and the most modern mill produced in 1913 only 32 tons per day." An increase in the size and turnout of mills and the scale of production is obviously very necessary as also improvement in quality and durability. Such improvements will go far to meet the objections of the printing trade.

The Chemical Industries.

The chemical industries present another special type of infant industry which possesses important peculiarities. Several industries of that group are what are called key industries and basic industries, while, further all these industries are inter-related in a most complicated manner. Thus, cheap sulphuric acid is not only important to industry but to agriculture, as it form the basis of many chemical manures; while Alkali industry forms the basis of the manufacture of soap and glycerine. Now, as originally formulated, the infant industry argument was applied only to manufactures of a finished character only. But further thought and experience have led to the extension of the argument to industries producing raw materials. Thus, Prof. Taussig observes that "so far as this special argument for protection is concerned there may be sometimes as good reason for duties on raw materials as on manufactures." There can be no doubt that government assistance of different kinds should be afforded to chemical industries, but as Sir P. C. Roy observes, "each manufacture will present a case which would have to be judged in co-relation with other manufactures to get at the real solution of improving the existing condition." There are special complications in the matter of framing a tariff for chemical industries, because of two factors which prevail in that group—so many of the chemicals are joint products and again some of them are the raw materials of numerous industries. In the case of the latter therefore the protection accorded in the shape of import duties should be in itself very moderate though it should be supplemented by assistance of another sort; otherwise the protection might stultify and make of no effect protection given to other industries. There is also the necessity of making a survey of our chemical resources before determining the exact rates of protection. Thus Dr. Sudborough and Simonsen have, for instance, expressed the view that "the amounts of tar available in India under present conditions are quite insufficient to start a large coal-tar industry". Such conditions of supply should be fully examined before the exact character of the protection to be afforded is decided in each case.

Complications of a tariff on Chemicals.

It is obvious that the infant chemical industry of India has its full share of initial difficulties. Its foreign rivals have the advantage of a great demand close at home. They also command better transport facilities, while the Indian chemical industries have to draw their raw materials from great distances. The growth of subsidiary industries in other countries is also very favourable to the foreign rivals. Then again, in some cases the raw material resources have not been developed as yet in India. Thus at present we depend on the imports of raw sulphur for the manufacture of our sulphuric acid. Some other countries like Great Britain manufacture the acid from Pyrites imported from Norway and Spain, but India has no facilities for direct importation from these countries. However, Sir P. C. Roy hopes that our abundant lower grade ores of Pyrites might be turned to account after suitable experiments.

We might be safely guided bv the views of eminent experts, like Sir P. C. Roy, who are of opinion that while in several directions in the case of chemical industries, protective tariffs will be useful, too much reliance should not be placed on them and other measures should also be employed to assist the development. As Sir Prafulla put it "the saving of a few per cents. by way of tariff-protection is very good, but cannot accomplish anything worth saying in the industries I feel keenly about." He insisted that the government should give *every variety of assistance* to the attempts, say, to cheapen sulphuric acid. Cheap acid will enable India to utilise its coal better by recovering the bye-products and it is not inconceivable that the whole range of tar-products might be open to us. The main instrumentalities which the state can employ are subsidies and guarantees to firms, cheaper railway freights and facilities as to leases. "A state-guaranteed or subsidised company situated in the vast fields of Jharia or still better in the recently discovered Talchar coal fields of Orissa with a spur running to the sea-coast for the manufacture of Brine and Alkali therefrom, thus making a chain of sulphuric acid tar products, alkali, would be quite a feasible project—provided the difficulties of leases and railway freights are smoothed over by the state." Such is the bold scheme of our foremost chemist.

His reasoning is supported as regards heavy chemicals by other chemists. Thus, Mr. Alcock told the commission that the chief centres of heavy chemical industries in England enjoyed the great natural advantage that they could draw their supplies of raw materials from a very small radius, and the same applies to the sale of their products and shipment for export. This advantage could be countervailed by having subsidised railway rates in India on raw material for the key-chemical industries. The Indian chemical industries are under a handicap because of the long freightage to bring our raw materials to centres where manufactures can find a market for the disposal of their products. In fact, the raw materials which are necessary for the heavy chemical industry are scattered all over the country. Of course care should be taken in granting such subsidised rates, not to give undeserved assistance to badly situated establishments. Each manufacturer should have to prove to a technical committee that he was reasonably entitled to such assistance.

Expert opinion before the Fiscal Commission emphasised that many branches of the Chemical industry were essential for the national security and of substantial importance to the economic prosperity of India. Thus, the manufacture of alkalis, nitrates, chlorine and of nitric and sulphuric acids; the isolation of aromatic hydro-carbons for the manufacture of explosives and the production of synthetic dyes would all have to be encouraged at some stage of the country's progress by the various means at the disposal of the state. This, of course, does not imply that protection should be atonce extended to all chemical industries; since it is most important to maintain a proper perspective in chemical development and progress. But, owing to the fact that the manufacture of heavy chemicals, chemical dyes etc. have been carried to a high pitch of perfection abroad state-help to our chemical industries is essential in some form and at some stage. In the case of incipient industries subsidies would be the most suitable method of assistance. But, above all, and even more than in the case of other industries any protection extended to chemical industries must be preceded by preliminary expert investigation of resources as well as potentialities; and, further, any future chemical tariff must be constantly regulated, supervised and altered under expert guidance.

Another infant industry of a basic character is the steel industry. The depression in the iron and steel industry is such that one need not be surprised that claims have been put forward in every country for some measure of protection. About 1919 the industry had reached its high-water mark ; but since then the production began to be unprofitable and in 1921 conditions became alarming in the leading manufacturing countries. Demand fell faster even than production, with the result that competition in export trade became keener and keener. These phenomena were accompanied by a fall of prices. The fall of prices in 1921 was continuous and was facilitated in the case of Great Britain and America by the reduction in the cost of fuel and by the adjustment of wages to the new conditions through the machinery of sliding scales. In these circumstances it was natural that the steel manufactures of India should ask for a certain measure of protection even of a temporary character. In fact, the situation on which the demand for protection was in itself more or less of a temporary character. In the first place, large quantities of cheap battle scrap were as they showed being used in Belgian and French furnaces. Again, they could point to the factories erected during the war as to the increased steel capacity of all the producing countries. This situation taken together with a fall in the home prices was a sure temptation to dumping. It was also alleged that countries like Belgium were giving bounties for every ton of steel exported. The example of other countries like America, Japan and France which had increased duties on imports of iron and steel was cited. For example, it was alleged that in Japan the duty had been raised to 10 per cent. on Pig-iron.

In studying this industry for tariff purposes we have to consider in the first instance what natural advantages it possesses.

Natural advantages and disadvantages of the Indian Steel Industry.

The basis of all progress in the industry must be the possession of adequate and suitable supplies of raw materials. India is very fortunate in possessing supplies of iron ore adequate for any probable increase of the present scale of manufacture in the country. There is controversy as regards the exact amount of the available supply and there is a very wide divergence of opinion between geologists on this point; but no one doubts that we have ore enough to serve as the basis of a much larger scale of production for a very long time. What is more, the ores is of very high quality, a good deal of it reaching a standard of 60 per cent. while in other countries the ore is worked as low as 28 per cent. It would be difficult to exaggerate the importance of this advantage. As a great authority on the iron industry has argued the iron ore problem is by far the most important, "first, because there is a much less ample supply of good iron ores than of good coal; and next, because while ½ ton of coal will usually suffice for the production of a ton of pig iron, the average consumption of ore is over two tons, and in a good many cases, including our own Cleveland district, Luxumburg, Alsace, and Alabama (U.S.) approaches, and even exceeds, 3 tons."* This has to be remembered as an encouraging consideration, the more so that we are not so fortunately circumstanced as regards our coal—a matter which will be discussed a little later. Another great advantage which we possess in one department of the industry—the production of pig-iron—is that we have got a great supply of cheap unskilled labour. Coming again to raw materials we find that we have large supplies of limestones but they are not close to the works. There is also a complaint that our limestone contains a less quantity of CaO than that of America, "the increased cost of calcining lime and the excess consumption is due to excess acid in the raw stone in this country and then we also have to calcine with a coal of inferior quality at higher cost." Thus neither the quality nor the location of the limestone supply can be said to be very satisfactory. Indeed, of late the quality of limestone and dolomite showed marked deterioration, but that was probably accounted for on other grounds.

---

*Jeans, *Iron Trade*, p. 10.

The Industrial Commission had expressed a doubt as regards the sufficiency of the supplies of good coking coal in India; further there is the opinion hazarded by the Imperial Mineral Resources Bureau that with the present rate of increase in extraction the known resources of 2,000 million tons of coking coal might be exhausted in forty years. These fears are very likely exaggerated. No doubt, Indian coal contains a higher percentage of ash, and a great deal of it is non-coking coal. So far our circumstances are less favourable than those of other countries. Fortunately however, this factor is balanced to some extent by the fact of the close proximity of our deposits of coal to those of the ore. Moveover experiments are being carried on in many countries for removing the ash from the coal by washing or mechanical separation. Germany which has been starved for fuel is also working in the direction of fuel economy. "Interesting experiments in low temperature carbonisation are being carried out by Mr. Ford, at present in America. If the process in successful it may alter the whole position as to the use of inferior coal in India." Thus though we must admit that we are up against a natural disadvantage at this particular point, we have the hope that after all it might turn out to be of a temporary and removable character.

As the sources of demand for the products constitutes a most important factor in the success of national industries we might glance at the present and potential market for steel in India. It could be said that our market in India is a growing one, and no doubt will ultimately form a very large market; still, just at *present* it cannot be asserted with accuracy that a country which consumes only about 700,000 tons annually forms a large market in any sense. In the great western countries the three leading heads of demand for steel are constituted by shipbuilding, railways and structural requirements. In India the first source of demand is conspicuous by its absence, while the structural use of steel is at present on a very limited scale. No doubt, however, there is a very promising field in the future for structural steel, when more steel will be used in urban buildings and when the ryot will largely extend his use of galvanised steel for domestic construction. Again, in the distant future, the potential use of better agricultural implements and the extension of irrigation will also enlarge its market. So also will the growth of the Engineering industries. All this however requires some decades. The railway demand will of course depend at any time on the rate at which railway development is pushed on. A moderate sized market, such, as we can command at present, will not afford very great scope for those economies of standardisation and specialisation on which a dominant steel industry of the modern type depends.

Among the disadvantages under which the industry is labouring at present might be mentioned the absence of any reserve of skilled labour comparable to those at the command of steel industries in other countries. At present "if a skilled man leaves us or is incapacitated, it takes six months and a large sum of money to replace him." Skilled and costly foreign labour has to be employed on special terms, at the same time that the corresponding quality of Indian labour is being trained up—a cumulative disadvantage. Moreover, such labour as we possess is not thoroughly domiciled. Climatic causes further account for the imperfect continuity of labour's services. "In other countries a man stands up with his face right up to the furnace all the year round, but here he cannot stand it for more than seven months. For the other months it is absolutely impossible for him to do it." How long this disadvantage will last is a matter of speculation. Our great steel manufacturers believe that "within fifteen years the practical disadvantages in cost would disappear." If might be that they are too optimistic. At any rate at present "our difficulties are chiefly caused by actual physical difficulties with the furnaces and the high cost of labour." Then again we have to import a number of materials from foreign countries.

It is remarkable however that the chief difficulties of an infant steel industry in our days remain insufficiently emphasised. Older foreign industries enjoy enormous advantages resulting from the progressive standardisation of products, the utilisation of bye-products, and the specialisation of particular establishments in certain branches of industry. Dr. Marshall thus illustrates the advantages of the enormous scale of production in America and Germany. "The metal can pass through many stages without ever getting cold ; waste gases can be used to generate horsepower to be applied directly, or through electricity ; and high chemical and other technical skill can find large scope in the supreme direction of many massive processes. Rolling mills, engine shops, etc., can often find occupation in slack times by enlarging and repairing their own plant, and that of the furnaces, and above all of the mines, and rails or plates, which happen to have been made unmarketable by slight flaws, can yet be turned to account in posts of no great responsibility about the mines, the furnaces, etc." Such are some of the advantages which an enlargement of the unit in the steel industry has brought in its train in other countries already, but indeed even greater economies are being expected from consolidation of the industry in future. We have the pronouncement of Lord Furness that in amalgamation lies the chief line of safety for the British Steel Industry. Nor are the advantages of large scale management yet exhausted. As organised competition from the United States, Germany, France and Belgium is increasing, the British iron—masters also are awakening to the possibilities of improved commercial organisation for export. When we compare or rather contrast such a vast scale of commercial organisation, industrial enterprise, labour power and command of material which form the might of the foreign industry, with our own weakness in every one of these respects, we come to the conclusion that although our disadvantages are removable, that consummation will take not only strenuous efforts but a long period of time.

Among the disadvantages of the local industry as presented by its representatives one at least appears to be over-emphasised, at least from the comparative point of view. The dislocation of railway services was asserted to be one of the main difficulties. No doubt it is so, in a sense, but then that difficulty is imposing an equal burden on the iron industries of all countries. Thus Mr. W. L. King, Vice-President of the Jones and Laughlin Steel Company, Pittsburg, observed before the Fordney Committee:—"The chief elements of cost to the American manufacturer is the increased charge for transportation. Generally speaking, it has more than doubled since the tariff of 1909, but you will, perhaps, better understand the effect on our costs by the specific statement that the cost of assembling the raw material per ton of steel in Pittsburg, and shipping the steel to New York where we must meet foreign competition is $10 per ton more than before the war." Similarly the increased freight charges are pressing heavily on the British Steel Industry. As the *Economist* observed in its issue of 17th February 1923, "while the selling price of steel is now only 25 per cent above the pre-war, railway rates still vary, from 60 per cent. to 200 per cent. above their old level for steel, coal, etc.," and further the burden of taxation is also very heavy. Mr. Peterson compared before the Tariff Board railways rates in India with ocean freights to India. In America and indeed in every country, the same complaint is to be heard. Thus it was asserted before the American Committee of Finance that while the railway freight per ton from Pittsburg to New York was over $7½ the ocean rate from England to that centre was less than $5½, while from Belgium or Germany to New York it was only $4½.

A comparative study of the costs of production at home and abroad must certainly form the true basis of any judicious tariff.

Cost Analysis of the Steel Industry.

But in this matter it is easy to expect too much from the proceedings of Tariff Boards. Comparative cost is a highly complicated and even ambiguous matter because much depends on how the accounts of industrial firms are classified. A thorough study of costs would require much more time and expense than is generally thought. Again a fair portion of the evidence must needs be taken in camera and this causes gaps and hiatuses when the student comes to a comprehensive study of the accounts published. Moreover, in the case of our own Tariff Boards, there were hardly any normal figures to compare—every aspect of the steel industry was hopelessly abnormal whether at home or abroad. It is to the credit of our Tariff Board, that in spite of these numerous difficulties and complexities an honest and strenuous effort was made to tackle the problem in the right spirit ; and the two or three sittings devoted to this analysis were rewarded by an amount of information on the topic, such as is not usually garnered in the proceedings of foreign tariff committees. The contrast must perhaps be due to the fact that our Tariff Board was as yet new to its work, ingenuous and unsophisticated, while in other countries the official tariff enquirers, with their much larger experience have long since despaired of getting hold of any really vital and relevent facts.

On the comparative side something was contributed by Mr. Tutwiler's comparison of the pre-war costs of producing steel in India and America. *Prima facie* it would seem that it would have been much more relevent and useful to obtain and compare present day figures for both countries ; but the fluctuations and abnormal conditions of industry in these days would have stood in the way of utilising such figures even were they available. As it is, when we are studying the comparison as it was actually instituted, we must allow on the one hand for the great rise of wages in the United States and on the other hand, for the economies which have been obtained of late years as the result of the great campaign for reducing the cost of production. Allowing for these important new factors, the comparison of the pre-war costs instituted by Mr.

Tutwiler is interesting as throwing light on our comparative advantages and disadvantages in production. Our limestone costs us more, and a larger supply of it has to be utilised while it is deficient in some important qualities. Some of our imported materials further increased our costs, while our coal also costs more than the American. We are also at a disadvantage in the matter of moulds and stools, but our greatest disadvantage is in the matter of labour cost per unit of steel production. For one thing, covenanted labour has to be imported on higher wages and better terms, while the Indian labour has also to be given attractive terms besides a month's leave every year. In America economy and efficiency of labour have been reduced to a science; the maximum efficiency of production is got out of labour by a widely diffused application of the premium system. America has also the advantage in possessing "a minimum range of standing charges; brought about by concentration of effort and policy on the problem of keeping works running full time,". Those who desire to study some of the merits of the American system in steel works might study with advantage Mr. J. S. Jeans's works on the Iron Trade.

As regards the potentialities and variations of the different elements of the cost of production of steel in India, much more information is rendered available by the evidence presented before the Tariff Board. The reasons for the increasing cost of production have been carefully analysed. In the first place, since the war there has been a rise in the price of coal from Rs. 3-13-0 a ton to Rs. 9-2-0 a ton. The cost of "feeding materials" has fluctuated considerably rising from 5.8 in 1916-17 to 6.4 in 1921-22 and then dropping to 4.15 in 1922-23. Even more serious is the fact that labour charges per ton have increased substantially. It is not that the average wages have risen in many departments—rather they have fallen in many branches of steel production. But, we have to employ more men per ton to get the outturn; in other words we are not getting the same result from the work done *per capita.* One reason assigned for this state of things was the fact that, in view of the extensions, more men are at present employed than are strictly necssary for the actual production; because the increased plant will only come into operation gradually and also because until the staff is trained they cannot get the full outturn of the plant. It might be pointed out that from the comparative point of view this handicap is not so serious as it would *prima facie* appear. Thus Mr. Buck, vice-President of the Bethlehem Steel Company, Pennsylvania, asserted before the Tariff Committee of 1921 that while American steel was selling at 66⅔ p. c. below the prices current in January, 1921 they were paying 54 per cent. more for labour than they did in 1913, with the costs of the steel close to the value in 1913. The general importance of the wages bill in the cost of production of steel was also fully brought out before that Committee; "while the labour cost per ton naturally varies with the various products, yet it is conservative to say as a general statement, that not less than 85 p. c. of the total cost of iron and steel products is labour."

The next item responsible for the increase in the cost of production of steel is constituted by the interest charges which have gone up by 528 p. c. between 1916-17 and 1921-22. This is due partly to the depletion of the reserves which the Tata Iron and Steel Company possessed in the earlier year. Further contributory factors are the need for increased working capital and the increased rate of interest which has to be paid in order to obtain this. An attempt was made to solve the difficult problem of allocating the total interest charge on the iron and steel produced; and expert opinion was in favour of ascribing a charge of Rs. 17-2 per ton of steel to the heading of interest charges.

On one who has not read much of the present day tariff

literature this account of the rise of the local cost of production might easily produce a feeling of disappointment. Even the able and well-informed President of the Tariff Board threw out the suggestion that "in most respect during the last six years progress has been retrograde, the quality of your materials has fallen off, and also the efficiency of your labour as judged by the output per man." The suggestion was of course thrown out in order to provoke discussion, but it was also based upon certain admissions. "Our materials—coal and feeding materials—decreased in quality during these years, we had to use 300 lbs. more coal per ton of ingot and coal rose from Rs. 4-12-0 a ton to Rs. 8-11-0. If our coal deteriorates in quality we cannot get the same production as we would get with better coal, that means more feeding materials." Such statements are certainly not of an encouraging character. Fortunately, there are other considerations, on the opposite side He who would properly judge the present condition of our industry, should have some idea of the general history of iron trade and of the extraordinary fluctuations of prices, costs and profits which have always been so prominent in the industry. Profits in the industry have varied largely from year to year in every country. As Mr. Jeans observes, "it is very surprising how long a business may be carried on without making any distribution of profits. In our own country cases are not unknown where no dividends have been paid for fifty years." In the United States steel industry, the fluctuation of profits and costs has always been very marked. Thus, between 1890 and 1900 the average cost of production for pig iron has varied from a minimum of 38*s*. to a maximum of 68*s*. In the single year 1901 the cost of steel rails varied from 86*s*. to 104*s*." But apart from these considerations, suggested by the history of iron trade, there are other factors to be taken into account. It has been suggested that in the case of the Tata Iron and Steel Industry "the reduction in the working cost in the next few years will depend not only on the efficiency of the new plant but also on the increased efficiency of the existing plant. It is hoped that a return might be made to the efficiency of the old plant in the next few years." There is no doubt that we should make a great effort to reduce our increased costs ; and nothing is so favourable to such an effort as a period of depression like the present. Thus, the great economies effected in the American Steel Industry at the end of the last century were mostly carried out in the period of depression from 1891 to 1893. The present slump also has witnessed great campaigns in other countries to reduce costs. In England, in 1922, a steady and continuous effort was made in this direction with the result that the selling price of steel was brought to only 25 p. c. above the pre-war level. "The sacrifice of the workers is sufficiently indicated by the fact that the average wage has been reduced from £5 7s. 11d. per week in 1920 to £2 17s. 8d. in 1922."* Germany has made important advances and researches in fuel economy. We are sure that fired by these examples, our own steel producer will not remain behind in the vital task of reduction of costs.

An exact analysis of the cost is rendered specially difficult in this particular case because we have to anticipate the effects to be produced in our costs by the projected extensions of steel works. This effect is expected be so marked as to have called forth a rather emphatic observation from Mr. Peterson: "If the greater extensions had not been erected the case for protection would be very much weaker, and it is really on the strength of the increased production that we are asking for protection." We are told further, that the new plant would be in full operation within six months and then the costs will come down. However, anticipations can only to a limited extent take the place of carefully estimated figures. It was admitted that the figures of Rs. 186 per ton of steel placed before the Tariff Board was an exceptionally high amount. It was added that "we have

The Economist, 17th February 1923.

given the actual cost, but it is exceptionally high." Indeed the difficulties in the way of stating anything like normal costs are very great, and insurmountable. The real difficulty about making a comparison is this: "we had barely started before the war. During the war we obtained great facilities in the matter of the traffic, we had no difficulty in disposing of our output which was taken by government. Between 1914 and 1918 it is very difficult to find a normal year. Control was taken off by government in 1920 and after that we had labour trouble." Such an absence of the means of determining normal cost both at home and abroad must render the task of the Tariff Board extremely difficult and complicated and must inevitably detract from the reliability and finality of its suggestions as to the rates of duty.

Factors affecting the amount of duty.

The problem of settling the amount of this duty and of settling up a steel schedule is not an enviable one, even under the most favourable circumstances: We have seen that there are abnormal variations of costs and prices everywhere, "but probably they reach their meridian in the United States, where yearlv differences of as much as 150 p. c. are not unknown, alike for iron ore, coke, pig iron and steel products."* Add to these standing difficulties, the abnormal features of present days and problem is rendered still more complicated. Nor are the manufacturers generally in the habit of assisting Tariff Boards by furnishing accurate or exhaustive data. Thus when the Fordney Tariff was on the *tapis*, the steel manufacturers addressed the Committee as this:—"Knowing the difficulty in securing accurate information as to foreign labour costs, efficiency and other conditions, and the uncertainty of the future, we are not able, even if disposed, to dispute your prognosis of the future as it may appear in this bill." Our own great steel manufacturing company has put forward a

*Jeans, "Iron Trade".

demand for a protective import duty of 33⅓ per cent. This is alleged to be based upon the prices of the English article landed in India (Rs. 150 per ton) compared with local cost of production of Rs. 200. We are not informed however over what period the alleged English price of Rs. 150 has prevailed, and in what sense it is to be regarded as a representative price. It is unfortunate that no questions were put to elucidate the grounds of this basic statement. It was considered that looking to all the circumstances "we should be able *under any conditions* to manufacture at that price for a considerable time." We have seen above that Rs. 186 was admitted to be "an exceptionally high cost"; so that we might take it that Rs. 200 a ton is a very liberal maximum, especially as we are assured that out steel producers can manufacture and sell at that price under any conceivable circumstances. But, it was also stated that this amount of protection is on the whole adequate only "against the ordinary rise and fall of prices." In case of heavy dumping or depreciation of exchanges additional protection was said to be necessary, and the representative of our great steel firm added the remark:—"I would prefer imposing a higher rate of duty from the start rather than to deal with it when emergency arises"—a commendable anticipation of all possible future troubles. It was also stated that the rate of 33⅓ p. c. was based upon estimates of cost for a period of five years and with that rate "we should be able to defy competition. It is impossible to see further ahead and after that period it may necessary to increase or reduce the duty." This idea of a fluctuating tariff is, however, one not to be recommended. Moreover, no attempt was made to relate and co-ordinate this demand for a 33⅓ rate with the statement of comparative cost presented later by Mr. Tutwiler. The proposed rate might be defensible although it looks *prima facie* too high; but it was not supported in the oral evidence by relevent figures. Perhaps it would have been better had a more moderate rate been proposed and had been backed up by a fuller statistical case. It might be that the higher figure actually brought forward was due to a certain misunderstanding. During some of the hearings the President of the Board repeatedly pointed out to the representative of the steel industry that neither interests nor profits could be calculated on what was set aside as depreciation. "If the sums written off are for depreciation in the ordinary sense, then before you attempt to ascertain what is the sum on which you are entitled to earn a profit, they must be deducted from the fixed capital expenditure." In a word "you must deduct depreciation before you take the capital on which you are going to calculate profits, otherwise you are calculating the same money twice over." Obviously, depreciation must figure either as cost or as capital expenditure but not in both capacities. Ultimately indeed, Mr. Peterson admitted the reasonable character of this suggestion. He observed :—"After reading the record of evidence I would alter my answer. I entirely agree with the President that if a full allowance for depreciation is made in the costing accounts, any sum set aside for real depreciation should not be taken into account in estimating the capital on which profit should be calculated as this has already been allowed for in the cost." Nevertheless, after making this admission the speaker did not perceive that, as a corollary, the rate asked for might be lowered. His general contention was that for an industrial enterprise to be considered reasonably successful it should yield 10 p. c. on the capital expenditure. In another place he urged, however that 15 p. c. would be a reasonable profit. "Capital cannot now be obtained for new industrial enterprises of this nature unless there is a fair probability that it will yield 15 p. c." As regards these statements, it might be pointed out, in the first place, that a very large capital has already been raised for the enterprise at a lower rate of interest ; and further that a great deal of the capital is being raised abroad at a much lower rate. Finally, the proposition before the Board was not sufficiently definite. It might mean that an *average* profit of 10 p. c. is wanted; or that a *minimum* of 10 p. c. is required; it might also mean that a 10 per cent. profit must needs be paid in periods of great depression like the present, in spite of the fact that the capital was raised to a considerable extent during periods of inflation. These are so many different propositions, and it is to be wished that the Board had put further questions to elucidate the exact nature of the main proposition.

The problem of calculating the necessary rate of profits is complicated in this particular case by the existence of certain prior contracts. It has been observed that under these contracts "the Tata Iron and Steel Company is committed to the annual supply of large quantities of rails at prices which, if accepted by English and Belgian companies, would be described officially by the Tata Company as an example of dumping". The question has also been raised whether with such contracts running on our great steel producing firm can reap the full benefits of any protection extended to it. In the discussion before the Board these objections were not directly met, but it was argued that, in general, the amount to be supplied under these contracts was not very large, and that in the case of some of the purchasing firms the Tata Iron and Steel Company owned a substantial share in their capital. It could also be added that a revision of these contracts was to be expected shortly; and further, that this lowering of prices was one way of giving a substantial discount to customers purchasing large amounts of the products of the Tata Company.

Several proposals were submitted in order to meet the abnormal competition from countries with depreciated exchanges. The first proposal was to ignore 25 per cent. of the depreciation and after that to increase the tariff automatically in proportion to the depreciation. Another proposition was that the English price should be taken as the basic price and the duty should be so fixed that the total price (including the duty) of the imported article landed in India should equal the price of similar material imported from England. As regards the first proposal, there is the difficulty that the exchanges are fluctuating and that in some cases the duty as projected would rise to extraordinary heights. To both schemes it might be objected that they would shut out much—needed imports, and finally that while they emphasise the advantages for exporting possessed by countries with depreciated exchange they ignore their disadvantages due to rising wages and costs. It cannot be supposed that while the external price of a country's currency goes on falling its internal price remains steady. A reference to the recent economic investigation on this subject might be recommended.

Dumping in steel.

One of the main supports of the demand for protection is the prevalance of dumping. The case put forward that India is the only market open to dumping in steel at present is no doubt an overstatement. It might have been argued with much greater effect that dumping—whether of the sporadic or of the permanent variety, must prove particularly injurious to an infant industry like the steel industry of our country. It ought further to be emphasised that there is a greater difference between the influence of dumping on a great exporting country like England and its action on a country like India of which the manufacturer depends mainly on the home market. In the former case where the country largely exports its steel products, dumping from abroad has its compensations, in as much as much of the dumped material is worked up for export to foreign countries. It has been recognized that the supply of dumped raw material has helped the English steel manufacturers, and has assisted the English steel producers to secure or retain foreign markets for finished goods. The disorganization of labour and capital caused by dumping must, on the other hand, exert a specially injurious influence upon a country beginning its manufacturing career. Thus it would appear that *the case for countervailing duties against dumping is particularly strong in the case of India.*

Unfortunately, no very satisfactory mass of proof was produced before the Tariff Board to support the allegations of dumping. The Board seemed far from satisfied with the amount of information placed at its disposal on the topics of dumping or of unfair competition assisted by bounties and subsidies. We can hardly proceed on an imperfect ascertainment of essential facts, and a full and careful inquiry in the matter of dumping is very necessary. Such an inquiry is rendered more difficult and exacting by the recent programmes of reduction in costs which have been carried out in so many countries. Mention has already been made of the steady and continuous efforts made by the English steel producers in this direction with the result that the producing costs have been brought down last year only about 25 per cent. above the pre-war level. Drastic reductions in wages might also lower costs to an extent which might arouse suspicion in the outsider. Nevertheless, after making ample allowance for all such factors, there remain many significant indications of dumping. Thus we read in the *Economist* of the 17th February, 1923, that "the bulk of the heavy steel produced in this country (England) is made at a heavy loss." The same journal observes as follows in its issue of the 3rd February of the same year :—"The natural step to take to revive industry is to reduce prices ; but in the case of the steel trade these had been so drastically cut in 1921 as to leave little room for further reductions in 1922. Further cuts were, however, made until *prices in many instances were substantially below actual costs.*" The same journal states in its issue of 17th November, 1923, that "orders have to be in many cases accepted at unremunerative prices and the financial results are by no means so good as the production figures might indicate." These are useful expressions indicating the course of prices in England. As regards America the steel manufacturers stated before the Select Committee on Finance, that in 1922 steel was selling at 66⅔ per cent. below the prices current in January, 1921. The freight costs were double what they had been before the war, and as regards supplies and materials necessary in steel production their prices had also risen hundred per cent. "Yet we are selling our product on practically a pre-war basis, hoping to stimulate a demand by cheapening our product." Even more striking and explicit was another statement made before the said Committee. "In fact to-day with pig-iron selling for 20 dollars, the maker does not realize enough cash to return him the cost of his raw materials and freight bills, he being out of pocket as to labor cost and overhead. What is true of pig-iron is likewise true of finished products made from pig-iron under the iron and steel schedule, *all of which are selling at several dollars per ton below cost of production*". No doubt, a full inquiry by the Tariff Board would produce much more evidence of dumping of steel; but those in charge of the inquiry should not fail to make allowance for the great reduction of costs referred to above. It is only after making such allowance that we can arrive at the real cases of dumping.

Burden of protection duties on steel.

The balance sheet of protection is a particularly complicated affair in the case of basic industries. The items on both sides of the account are much larger and more numerous than in the case of other industries. For example, if protection is to be given to the steel industry in the form of import duties, the country must be prepared to shoulder a great burden. The representative of the industry admitted it himself in general terms. "We realise however that until Indian works are in a position to supply that total requirements of India there will always be some difficulty in imposing so high a tariff." This was a wise and far-sighted admission ; for few countries are in the unenviable situation of being called upon to initiate such a movement towards protection at a time when iron and steel have become the materials *par excellence* of every conceivable industry, and when their price forms a very substantial part of most articles. In a word, we are faced with the problem of protecting steel in *the very heart of the iron age.* Even among basic industries, iron and steel form a class by themselves. If protection is afforded to them through import duties the result will be either that a great many other industries—almost all nascent ones in the case of India—will be handicapped, or that compensating protection must be afforded to all of them for at least a generation or two. For nothing in the tariff history of any country prepares us to accept the common view that in a decade or so the steel industry could be made self-supporting; it took America thirty years to become self-supporting in the matter of steel rails alone. Many of the industries which will thus be handicapped are younger even than the steel industry, *e.g.*, the engineering trade; on the other hand some are very old and feeble, *e.g.*, our agriculture. To say this is of course not the same thing as to assert that protection should not be extended to steel; the statement is however particularly relevent us to the problem of the shape in which that protection is to be given—whether is is to be given in the form of bounties or of import duties. That problem necessitates some indication of the nature and aspects of the burden. There is no difficulty in perceiving that in granting substantial protectionist duties to steel we are entering upon a vista of *a series of conflicts* between basic industries. The coal industry is essentially a basic industry of which the importance cannot be exaggerated ; and there can be no doubt that our collieries will be seriously handicapped by the rise in the prices of the steel products essential for their operations. Protective duties on steel will reduce our steel imports but also will increase our coal imports by handicapping our collieries in their efforts to retain the domestic market. Already the foreign coal has effected a lodgment in our market, and if we artificially enhance their cost of replacing coal machinery, depreciation allowances, etc., foreign imports of coal will no doubt assume a dominant position. The collieries will be also hit by the increase of railway rates which must follow from an increase in the price of steel. The fact is that the great basic industries like the steel industry, the coal industry and transportation are most intimately interwoven, and we cannot touch the fabric of one of them without causing serious reaction on the others. With a rise in the price of steel—and therefore of its product machinery—our annual capital railway expenditure of so many crores annually would be very substantially augmented to the detriment of the taxpayer. As it is, we have put up our rates very high, and still we are not out of the period of railway deficits. Moreover, it is at present imperative not only to push forward new construction but to make good the depreciation brought about during the war period. It needs scarcely be pointed out that the steel industry itself has been a great sufferer from the railway disorganisation and the rise of freights. Mr. Peterson was asked by the Tariff Board how the railway disorganisation had raised the cost of production of steel. He answered: "it is chiefly in the cost of coal. We consider that the present high cost of coal is an artificial price caused largely by the shortage of waggons." It was explained further that the amount of coal demanded by our industries cannot at present be handled by the railways and that the effect of the railway disorganisation is that the supply of coal is short and that hence the price rose high. The higher prices of steel coal and transportation will affect adversely every other Indian industry. Thus, the agriculturist will have to pay higher price for his implements, because the producers of agricultural machinery will require compensating protection; the manufactures of galvanised sheets will similarly increase the prices of a material which is now so largely used in the construction of the peasants' dwellings. Among other things, the agriculturist will be affected by any increase in the cost of the construction of irrigation works, and one has only to remember the immense potentialities of irrigation in India. The Port Commissioners have emphasised before the Tariff Board that they utilised steel "for an unusually large number of purposes" and in ways which demand varying degrees of fabrication. They asserted that the proposed tariff on steel would entail a great additional burden on them. They pressed for the exclusion of fabricated structural steel at least from the proposed tariff, since otherwise "all plants imported into India, a great part of which cannot now be produced in this country would be enhanced in cost, the effect of which would be extremely serious." It might have been added that any great increase in the price of structural steel would tend to emphasise the stagnation of our building operations and would affect adversely the numerous occupants of our urban houses flats and mansions.

Some idea of the compensating duties which would be claimed if protection on ordinary lines is given to steel can be obtained from the evidence of Mr. T. Gavin Jones, President of the Upper India Chamber of Commerce, who appeared before the Fiscal Commission as representing the Mechanical Engineering trade. He agreed that iron and steel trade should be assisted by import duties but he wanted much higher duties to be put on the manufactures of the finished articles made from steel. Accordingly he suggested a tariff on the following lines:—

	Per cent.
Pig-iron	2½
Iron and Steel, wrought	7½
Machinery generally	15
Textile machinery	10
Agricultural machinery	5
Railway plant	15

He was of opinion that the steel industry would not require even a 20 per cent. duty or anything like it ; but he insisted that, if a

30 per cent. duty was given to it he would add 30 per cent. at least to his other requirements as stated above. His idea was that lower rates should be given to textile machinery because we are not likely to be able to manufacture it in the near future ; on the other hand, railway plant could be manufactured in India now and it should be developed as rapidly as possible; consequently it coul justly claim a higher duty.

It is obvious from the above considerations, that any protection given to the steel industry should be both moderate and essentially temporary so as not to obstruct the development of other industries. In connection with this conflict of interests, a suggestion thrown out by Sir Campbell Rhodes and accepted by several expert witnesses before the Fiscal Commission deserves consideration. It is to the effect that the same flat rate of duty should be imposed upon the products of the basic industry and of the finishing industries. Thus to take an illustration, a 15 per cent. duty might be put on steel, machinery, railway plant and rolling stock ; this will adjust in an equitable way the claims of all these industries for protection. The steel industry would in the result obtain a protection of 15 per cent. The industry making machine tools will not be hampered much, because, although it has to pay 15 per cent. more on all the steel it uses, yet the cost of steel is only a small part of its total cost of production. Supposing for the sake of example, that the cost of steel formed one-tenth of the total cost of the machine tool (of course in practice it will form a much smaller proportion) the machine tool industry under this scheme loses 1½ per cent. but obtains a protection of 15 per cent. *i.e.*, it has a net protection of 13½ per cent. Needless to say that all the figures used in this illustration are purely hypothetical.

It was the certainty of these endless conflicts of interest

between industries which would be the necessary consequences of the required heavy steel tariff that led the Fiscal Commission to recommend bounties as the better way of assisting basic industries. This view can be supported both on theoretical and practical grounds. On the theoretical side it would be difficult to apply the young industry argument validly to a particular industry at the cost of keeping back the development of numerous nascent industries—many of them also key industries. Again in the present keen international competition the laurels will remain with that country which can soonest reduce its costs of production. Now, it is well known that bounties afford a much greater stimulus to the reduction and lowering of costs. The public-spirited management of the Tata Iron and Steel Company have always highly appreciated the superior advantages of a bounty:—"In our original application to government we suggested that the assistance required by the industry could best be given in the form of a bonus on production, and we would still *prefer* that a moderate duty of, say, 15 per cent. should be levied on foreign steel and the balance of the protection required should be afforded by means of a direct bonus on production, the financial assistance required being obtained from the proceeds of the duty suggested." The demand cannot be described as unreasonably high as starting point of a careful investigation, though impartial study by the Board must lead to a tangible alteration of the figures proposed. From the point of view of steel producers themselves, it can be easily seen that bounties are preferable to duties. There is no industry in which the economics of massive production and of multiform standardisation are so important as in the steel industry. A large and rapid increase in home consumption is essential for the continuous prosperity of our steel industry. The greatness of the American steel industry was made possible by the increase of consumption of steel *per capita* from

Case for bounties.

20 lbs. to 500 lbs. within less than half a century. The development of economies in the industry assumes the growth of other industries which furnish the market of its products. Hence it is not in the permanent interests of the steel industry that other industries should be kept back by a rise in the price of their principal raw material—steel. The representative of our steel producers was therefore wise in expressing his preference for bounties. No doubt, protectionist import duties would enable the Tata Iron and Steel Company to continue to exist, but bounties would help them to develop into greatness. This consideration is the more important in India, since our industries are few and young, and in no position to bear the heavy burdens of a rise in the price of steel, of coal and of transportation.

There is another reason why bounties would prove more attractive to our steel manufacturers than import duties. Having asked for temporary protection they had to propose a gradual reduction of the import duty in about fifteen years. But, as is well-known, the gradual reduction of import duties might affect protection in unexpected and uncertain ways. Under conditions of continuously falling prices a reduction of the duty might abnormally stimulate foreign import, especially if the duty is *ad valorem*, whereas with a bounty on production the protection to the industry is certain even though being reduced by stages.

From the national point of view also, under the circumstances there are special facilities and conveniences for the use of bounties. We have to deal with only two or three great individual establishments in the industry which are ably managed and cannot be accused of any want of zeal for industrial development. They themselves have asserted their preference for bounties. We have also special facilities for giving indirect bounties, as has been suggested; there might be a guarantee of government orders for a term of years, the price to be based on the costs of the Tata Iron and Steel Company; the railways too might contribute their share to the bounty by revising generously their contracts with the Tata Iron and Steel Company. By a resort to such methods the direct burden of the bounties on our Treasury might be reduced. It has been seen how the indirect sacrifices required by the application of protection to ordinary industries are multiplied in the case of basic industry; and how the argument in favour of bounties (as against import duties) is weighted and made much stronger in these cases. This combination of the theoretical and practical advantages on the side of bounties has led several countries in recent years to utilise bounties on iron and steel production. Thus in Australia by the Iron and Steel Products Act of 1922, the following bounties are to be paid unless the profits of manufacture already exceeds 15 per cent. per annum on the capital employed.

Fencing Wire	... ...	£2-12 per ton.
Galvanised Sheets	... ...	£2-12 ,,
Wire netting	... ...	£3-8 ,,

It might be added that at the same time the import duties were reduced to some extent. In New Zealand the Iron and Steel Act of 1914 which set aside £150,000 for the payment of royalties of 12s. per ton for pig iron, puddled bar iron and steel produced from bar iron and 24s. per ton for steel produced direct from the furnace in New Zealand has been extended to the year 1931. South Africa has fixed bounties to be paid in respect of pig iron and steel produced in the Union. The bounty consists of 1s. 6d. a ton for the first three years, 15s. per ton for the next three years and they are then annually reduced by 2s. 6d. a ton till the payment of bounty ceases after eleven years.

The proposed Indian system of bounties might well be something along these lines, although there is no reason in our case why the bounties should be raised gradually. It was necessary in those Dominions to begin slowly in order to see whether a substantial amount of production would respond to the offer of bounties. In the case of India there is no such necessity because the Iron and Steel industry has already showed its capacity for growth during the war and has asserted its claim to be supported through an epoch of temporary difficulties by means of bounties.

Lessons of anti-dumping legislation.

The experience garnered by the United States Tariff Commission ought to be of high value to us in India, both as regards the proper attitude to be observed by the inquirer in the matter of dumping, and as regards the right lines of anti-dumping legislation. That commission regards the existence of "a tendency to complain indiscriminately, not only of those methods condemned everywhere as unfair, but also of every form of successful foreign competition." It refuses to accord its sanction to such complaints of dumping, because encouragement given to such suggestions would upset legitimate business and would provoke retaliation abroad. It suggests some *criteria of dumping* which should indicate when price-cutting could be said to amount to dumping. "Ordinary price-cutting and underselling are so universal, both in domestic and foreign fields, that it is taken for granted that restrictions are contemplated only when their practice is accompanied by *unfair circumstances or by unfortunate public consequences.*" Our inquirers into the phenomena of dumping would do well to bear in mind these criteria. They should investigate whether the price-cutting is accompanied by either unfair competitive devices or by injury caused to our industrial development. A useful commentary upon the dictum of the Commission is furnished by the Australian legislation on dumping. That law would guard against such foreign competition as would lead to the curtailment of production in Australia or to the labour employed in Australian industries being remunerated inadequately.

To do justice to the Indian steel producers, it must be added, that their representative before the Fiscal Commission regarded foreign competition in a wise and tolerant spirit. Regarding the fact that in some cases the export prices of American and German goods are lower than the home prices he remarked:—"I don't know whether I can call it dumping. It is an endeavour to sell in the market outside at a lower price. There is nothing unreasonable in it. We should also do it if we had a chance." It is, indeed, not unlikely that Indian pig-iron has been sold abroad on occasions at a lower price than it commanded at home. On the other hand, all will agree that it is not necessary, in order to prove dumping, to establish any actual intention to injure, destroy or prevent the establishment of a domestic industry. Such an intention cannot be said to form an essential element of dumping. The ordinary motive of the typical dumper is only to sustain his production at its full capacity by disposing of his surplus stocks abroad at low prices.

As we in India have had, so far, little experience of anti-dumping legislation, it is instructive to glance at some of the difficulties of such legislation as well as to indicate some of the methods employed and suggested with the object of making it a success from the point of view both of the domestic producer and consumer. To take an example, it is generally admitted that the Canadian anti-dumping ilaw has been a success; but then the administrators of that measure enjoyed the great and peculiar advantage of close geographical proximity to the United States whence the dumping mainly orginated. As a consequence, they enjoyed great facilities for procuring dependable information as regards the domestic values of the dumped goods. Had the Canadian law been directed chiefly against dumping from overseas the task would have been far more complicated owing to the complexity of world-wide foreign prices of imported articles This is indeed, one of the main difficulties of anti-dumping legislation—how to secure information as to the values placed on the dumped goods in their home market. With the object of getting over this difficulty the government of the United States deputed special customs officers to Europe. In any particular case referred to them, they would visit the exporter and request full information as regards his prices. If the exporter declined to give such information the dumping duty was applied to his goods. There are further complications to be reckoned with. Great skill is required to fix the dumping duty at the proper level. It must not be higher than what is strictly necessary, because then there would be differential taxation which might injure the domestic consumer. On the other hand, it must be high enough to prevent dumping. For as Prof. Dietzel has put it, low duties "afford no security that the flood due to over production in other countries will not wash over the tariff wall." One has to consider carefully not only the effects of the proposed duty on the supplies actually dumped into our country, but on the scale of production abroad and thus on the foreigner's potentialities of dumping. Care should also be taken as regards the selection of the proper type of duty employed. It has been urged by Dr. T. E. Gregory that "If the duty is *ad valorem* and not specific the danger of dumping is greater from the standpoint of the protected area than from that of the unprotected." The reason is that with *ad valorem* duties, the lower the price placed by the dumper on his goods, the less he has to pay. In a word, a premium is placed on intensive and heavy dumping.

The chief lesson to be derived from the anti-dumping legislation of Canada consists of the methods in which it has tried to prevent the law from needlessly raising prices to the consumer. Thus, the law is limited in its application to goods "of a class or kind produced in Canada." Even so, it has been observed with justice that its provisions should not have been extended to articles on which otherwise there are no duties, *i.e.*, those admitted duty free. There are other provisions of the Canadian law which make for the required elasticity in its application and administration. "Some consequences of too sweeping an enactment were avoided in Canada by the provision that the minister of customs by regulations may allow the temporary exemption of goods from the dumping duty, if the minister is satisfied that similar articles are not made or sold in Canada in substantial quantities to all purchasers on equal terms under like conditions." This provision is directed against monopolistic tendencies in the domestic industry. There are other articles as regards which a temporary exemption of their imports from the anti-dumping duty has been provided for—when the difference between the fair market value abroad and the selling price to the importer is only a small per centage of the fair market value. All these provisions tend to prevent an *undue* increase to domestic consumers of the prices charged for imports ; and the United States Tariff Commission has recommended the drafting of similar elastic provisions in the case of anti-dumping legislation in their own country. In the same spirit, it must be remembered in India, that the object of anti-dumping laws is merely to check dumping, and not to grant indirectly or incidentally an instalment of unnecessary protection nor to extend preference to the wares of any country.

A comparison of the Canadian legislation and that of the United States on the subject leads to the conclusion that administrative remedies to prevent dumping are superior to the penal method—of penalising and punishing the dumper. Under the American Act of 1916 the dumper was pronounced guilty of a misdemeanour and might be fined and even imprisoned. Experience showed however that a good deal of what could fairly be termed dumping could not be brought within the scope of the law and the exactitude both of legal language and procedure made it extremely difficult to secure convictions. Australia has so far improved upon the American model that on a complaint of dumping being certified by the Comptroller-General, the Minister might refer the matter for the decision of a judge.

Publicity is secured by the provision "that the judge shall sit in an open court". "He shall be guided by good conscience and the substantial merits of the case, without regard to legal forms or technicalities, or whether the evidence before him is in accordance with the law of evidence or not." He can prohibit the importation of the article or allow it subject to restrictions and limitations. In any case, it is advisable that some judicial or, better still, a quasi-judicial and expert committee should be vested with the jurisdiction to investigate and report upon specific complaints of dumping. In India we have the Tariff Board which can be utilised for this purpose.

Our survey of anti-dumping legislation abroad has provided us with some lessons which might prove of value to India. Should anti-dumping legislation be contemplated, great care should be taken in laying down the true criteria and distinguishing marks of dumping. As far as possible the legislative provisions might be made of such an elestic character as to prevent an unnecessary increase of prices to domestic consumers. The business of ultimately pronouncing on the existence of dumping should rest not with administrative officials solely but with an expert body which should not be unduly tramelled by legal technicalities. Apart from this, however, considerable discretion should be left with administrative authorities, who should also be supplied not only with specialist appraisers at home but with investigating agents to conduct enquiries into prices abroad.

Indian glass-industry: its advantages and difficulties.

The history of glass industry in India is remarkable, both for the uniform failure of the earlier experiments and for the tenacity with which, undeterred by these failures, more industrialists have embarked on fresh experiments. At present there are over twenty glass-works in India.

The advantages which have steadily attracted such enterprise are obvious. As regards the sand and lime used in the manufacture, fairly satisfactory qualities are readily available, although there is some evidence that the sand and coal obtained in continental countries for the same purpose is of a superior quality. Again, labour in India is cheap and readily obtainable. It might also be added that the natural protection enjoyed by the local industry is unusually great—glass being both a heavy and a fragile article. India presents to the imports of glass the disadvantage of long distances, while it affords to the comparatively small local establishments the benefit of markets in their near vicinity. The industry obviously enjoys a great deal of natural protection.

But, as is the case with every infant industry, there are initial difficulties to be reckoned with. Its foreign rivals can produce a cheaper output on account of the advantages of larger and better organised factories, efficiently trained labour, long experience and the employment of labour-saving machines. They have the benefit, for example, of automatic blowing and pressing machines. If the local industrialist tries to purchase such machinery he has to pay a very high price because such price has to cover the payment for patent and royalty. It is also to be noted that some of the chemicals both for colouring or purifying glass, as well as one of the three basic materials, namely soda ash, have to be imported, although the establishment of the soda ash industry in India might in future reduce this handicap. One of the great difficulties is that of training skilled hands. Indeed, it was argued before the Fiscal Commission that the difficulty of training new hands would itself countervail a protectionist duty of 25 per cent. The local cost is also increased by the necessity of employing glass technologists, a measure which is very necessary because as the Indian Industrial Commission observed "the glass-indusrty, even in its simplest form, is highly technical and can be efficiently carried on only by scientifically trained managers and expert workmen. The present state has been reached by importing men, only partially equipped with the necessary qualifications from Europe and Japan." Then again, there are difficulties relating to the design and construction of furnaces and the manufacture of crucibles and pots. The making of crucibles has not been locally taken up at all, while the complaint has been made that the crucibles from Japan are costly and not very satisfactory. Finally the location of some at least of the factories has not been selected with conspicuous skill. Sir Alfred Chatterton observes that "the sites for most factories have initially been selected regardless of the fact that the assemblage of the raw materials would involve heavy transport charges." Indeed, such mistakes are only to be expected when an industry is in its infant stage, when the economies of its industrial siuation have yet been imperfectly studied and when there are so many complex considerations to be taken into account in selecting a proper locality. Different situations might appear suitable according as we take into account vicinity to the fuel coming from coalfields, or proximity to the source of the required sandstones, or nearness of market, or availability of labour. Other matters, too, have to be looked into ,like distance from the seaboard where foreign competition would be greatest. Other authorities besides Sir Alfred have emphasized the necessity of greater foresight in the selection of sites for glass works in India. Thus in his "Notes on Glass Manufacture" Mr. C. S. Fox writes: "A large number of the existing glass works in India have been erected without sufficient attention to their normal working economy. In some instances the raw materials and coal are brought long distances by rail. In other factories due consideration has not been given to the variety of glassware in the greatest demand in the neighbourhood of the works. Consequently, the result has been that either the cost of production is high or the freight charges on the finished goods are heavy."

In spite of these difficulties, the Indian Glass industry can claim to have made satisfactory progress. Labour has been trained for the ordinary work of blowing. Again, we now possess men trained in the work of the construction of ordinary types of furnaces and in the mixtures and recipes for making ordinary glass. We might be said to be successful in producing the simpler kinds of glassware, such as globes, chimneys, tumblers, bottles, and coarse bangles. On the other hand, as has been said, we are still lacking furnace or chemical experts of real merits, and it can be added that there are very few trained managers in the industry.

Progress achieved by it.

Undoubtedly, the industry deserves to be assisted by the state. This help can be rendered in a number of ways. A great many authorities recommend the erection and working of a government glass factory. The functions of this factory should consist of developing the technology of glass manufacture in India and of training up experts and managers for the local glassworks. This function cannot be left even to a subsidised private factory since such an establishment would naturally attach more importance to profits than to experimental work. Another direction in which assistance might be found to be suitable on inquiry, would be by allowing a specially low classification to glass in transit. On this point too all experts are agreed. A special reason for this transport concession appears to exist in the case of glass. Sir Alfred Chatterton points out that railway rates are charged on gross weights and the ratio between the net weight and gross weight of glass packed for transport is usually very low. It is also alleged that recently the railways have raised the basis for calculation of weights for a waggon-load. For example, for a waggon of 16 tons, they formerly took the basis for calculation at 81 maunds the goods being bulky ; at present they take at 120 maunds. It is also to be noted that freight by steamer is

Methods of assisting glass-industry.

much lower than the railway freight which the local manufacturer has to pay. If after assistance has been granted along such lines it is felt that more help is necessary moderate import duties might be considered, the reason for keeping protection in this direction at a moderate level being that the local factories can supply a very small fraction of the total demand of the country and under such circumstances to put a heavy import duty would be to burden the consumer unduly. Much discrimination should also be used in applying the proposed protection to the proper grades of glassware. It is a fallacy of ambiguity that the infant industry argument compels us when helping an industry to help every grade of it. In any case, as regards glass manufacture many of the higher stages can hardly be said to exist, and we are not yet manufacturing to a tangible extent—sheet or plate glass or table glass.

The desirability of protection to the sugar industry has been recently engaging the attention of the Indian Sugar Committee. The application of tariff assistance in this direction is perhaps the most complicated problem which the Indian protectionism has to face. In general, protection is employed to overcome difficulties of the manufacturing phase. But the difficulties in the way of the Indian Sugar Industry are manifold being partly connected with the land-system, partly with the methods of agriculture and partly with the system of manufacture. We can thus perceive what an abnormally heavy task will be set to protection when it is called upon to make the sugar industry a success in India. The agricultural handicap is itself of a formidable character. Mr. Wood of Messrs. Parry and Co. told the Indian Fiscal Commission that assistance should be given in the way of nursing the raiyat and teaching the raiyat to grow the right kind of cane. He also observes that unless India can grow cane in large blocks it can never produce sugar cheaper than the foreigner. This evidence was

Problems of the sugar industry.

supplemented by that of Mr. Shakespeare, an eminent expert representing the Indian Sugar Producers' Association. He observed that there were certain natural disadvantages under which the Indian industry sucers. Of these disadvantages the greatest is "the climate. The growing period is very short. We have a dry cold winter, then a very hot spell, then very heavy rain and then cold again. I am speaking of Northern India. The climate is much more equitable in the South, in the Peninsula. But taking Northern India it is very far from being an ideal cane-growing climate. . . . If we get the field-yield that Java does, I do not think there will be any question of protection." Similarly, the Indian Sugar Committee of 1920 ascribed much of the superiority of Java in the matter of producing sugar to the methods of cultivation and to the efficiency which has been brought to bear on the agricultural side of the sugar industry. Mr. B. J. Padshah also in his brilliant supplementary note to the report of that Committee emphasises the necessity of organised improvement in present cultivation. He would trust to science and capital to make up for the deficiencies of soil and climate; Much also depends on improvements on the side of land-tenure. "If the system of land-tenure in the country permit the putting up of large factories and if the requisite enterprise, capital and science be forthcoming, the modern method of attacking the sugar problem would in India without the addition of a single acre of cane-lands and without any improvement in the methods of cultivation continue to give the present supply of *gur* and add 700,000 tons of white sugar to the production of the country without extra cost." The majority of the Committee, too, laid the greatest stress on agricultural improvement. Thus its "recommendations throughout have been aimed at securing the extension of cane-cultivation and, what is far more important, the adoption of improved methods both of cultivation and of manufacture. . . . . We fear that any increase in the duty might result in bolstering up an inefficient industry to the detriment of the consumer; and that secure behind the high protective wall factories in India might make no effort to reach the standard of those in other sugar-producing countries, notably in Java, where the industry has been able to dispense with any protection subsidy or assistance from the government." Without going so far as the Committee, we can with advantage note that the soundness and development of the sugar industry is largely a question of agricultural organisation and method. Before the Indian Fiscal Commission Mr. Shakespeare himself has accounted for the superiority of Java in the sugar industry by pointing to "the climate, the fertility of the soil, and the wonderful organisation of industry. It is one of the best organised industries of the world. They spend an enormous amount of money on the industry,—not the government, but the industry itself."

We might now turn to consider the proposals made as regards the amount of tariff-protection by the experts representing the sugar interest. Their view was that "under the present conditions the industry would require *permanent protection*." If, indeed, it is added, conditions improve and the cost of production is greatly reduced the protection might perhaps not be permanent. But this reduction of cost of production is "bound up to a great with what the Government is able to do in the direction of growing cane. It is mostly on the agricultural side that we are so far behind." In fact Mr. Shakespeare's evidence emphasises at every step that it is agricultural development which is wanting and he would invoke protection, in order to remedy this weakness. He goes on to add:—"On the manufacture side, I think we come fairly close to Java; but on the field side we are a long way behind, and that is of course the most important side of the industry really."

This line of reasoning implies that the state should start by assisting the sugar industry with heavy protection (33⅓ per cent.

has been proposed by Mr. Shakespeare). The state should then attempt to improve agricultural conditions and tenures, and since this is likely to be a very long-period affair the claim is put into permanent protection. It was also asserted that "even if a permanent duty is maintained and the cost to the consumer is increased, it would be to the national advantage of India to develop the industry." It should be noted that while the experts had claimed a duty of twenty per cent. before the Indian Sugar Committee, they raised the proposal to 33⅓ per cent. before the Fiscal Commission.

It is interesting to enquire how far the Sugar Industry of India benefited by the increased prices and higher tariffs of the post-war period. As the Indian Sugar Committee observe "the present duty affords a very substantial measure of protection to the Indian Sugar industry". Nevertheless the industry has not been able to take full advantage of the stimulus on account of the then existing difficulty in obtaining new machinery. It was also noted that companies registered in the United Kingdom lost any benefits that might have been accrued by the high prices owing to the operations of the British Excess Porfits Tax. In a word, the conditions were so abnormal that the benefits of the additional protection could not be secured. Moreover, even the period following the war has presented abnormal features and disturbed conditions. As the Indian Sugar Committee has pointed out, in a single year sugar has been quoted in New York at as high a rate as 23 cents per lb. and at as low a rate as 7 cents; estimates for a thousand ton sugar factory were quoted at £220,000 in one month of the year and at £350,000 in another month of the same year. During the same year the price paid by the Upper India Factories for their cane rose from 4½ annas to 12 annas per maund. With such an accumulation of disturbing factors it is naturally difficult to trace the effects of high prices and increased duties.

Opinions are far from agreed as to the effects which a

protectionist duty might have in the way of burdening the consumer. There is of course no doubt that the consumer of the refined sugar must pay a higher price under a protectionist regime; the question, however, is how far the duty on sugar is likely to affect the price of *gur*. Mr. Shakespeare argued that "eating *gur* has a separate market of its own. These *gurs* do not fluctuate to the same extent as what we call refined sugars. When refined sugar was at a very low rate, eating *gur* was selling at a very special price. They are sweetmeats and they are eaten in the form of *gur*." On the other hand, there were experts on the Bombay side who expressed the view that "if the protective duty is imposed on foreign sugar, the first effect will be the rise in price of *gur*." It is difficult to decide where doctors disagree. But general economic considerations would show that import duties generally raise the price not only of the imported article but of its local substitutes. We do not imply that the price of refined sugar and of *gur* will rise by exactly the same amount. Allowance must be made for differences of quality; but there can be no doubt that the protective duty on sugar must raise the price of *gur*; and any rise in price of *gur* implies that we shall be taxing an enormous number of consumers for the benefit of a comparatively small industry.

Burden of protection to the consumer.

In the same connection a question has been raised whether the beneficial results of protection to refined sugar as regards the national interests in general are not being exaggerated. As Mr. Sahasrabuddhe, the representative of the Bombay Agricultural Graduates' Association argued, the object of putting import duties is to discourage import of those manufactures for which the raw material exists in the country and is either wasted or exported. But in the case under consideration although the raw material is produced in the country it is more than fully utilised. The *gur* is a perfectly healthy and good article for human consumption and there is no special advantage to the country in turning *gur* into sugar. It must be admitted that there is much to be said for the views of Mr. Sahasrabuddhe. But regard is to be had on the other hand to the fact that India is importing increasing and enormous quantities of refined sugar. This implies that the class of consumers which would use refined sugar rather than *gur* is increasing and also that the standards of consumption are changing. Moreover India is capable of producing enough cane not only to supply the present consumption of *gur* but also to feed large manufactures of refined sugar. There is undoubtedly a case for encouraging sugar manufacture by all judicious means.

An accumulation of difficulties.

A great deal of hesitation will naturally be felt before extending protection to the sugar industry. The first consideration that will strike the enquirer is that the protection claimed is very high and even if it is not permanent, it will have to endure for a very long time. Then again the nature of the difficulties in the way of the development of the industry is such as to render it unlikely that they could be removed by protection. The problem is, as we have stated above, mainly an agricultural one. The sub-tropical climate of Northern India, its system of land-tenure and the fragmentation of holdings are the main difficulties which make an extension of the system of large factories difficult. It cannot be said that protection can with advantage be employed to remedy such an accumulation of difficulties. Then again, Java has some other advantages of a less desirable sort. The sugar-manufacturer there is able to sell cheap because he is enabled to control both the agriculturist and the labourer. It can hardly be supposed even by the stalwarts of protectionism that protectionist assistance will be able to counterbalance all these advantages. A further difficulty has to be faced in extending protection to this industry in the shape of the abrupt and extraordinary fluctuations in the world-price of sugar ; as a necessary consequence of these any protection afforded to the industry will also have to be an exceptional and varying character.

LECTURE VI.

PROTECTION AND FOREIGN CAPITAL.

Highest authorities—protectionist or free trade—favour free entry of foreign enterprise and capital.

It was perceived very early in the history of protectionism that one of the fundamental conditions of the success of any experiment on that line was the admission and utilisation of foreign capital and organising power. A series of high authorities could be quoted in favour of this view, ranging from List who imparted its present character to the protectionist theory to writers of the same side who are our contemporaries. One of Lists' criticisms of Adam Smith is to the effect that "he has not taken into account, that by the policy of favouring native manufacture a mass of foreign capital, *mental as well as material*, is attracted into the country."* List emphasizes the peculiarly advantageous position occupied by the United States of America as regards the adoption of protection owing to the fact that they could depend more than any other nation on attracting to themselves English capital, artificers, men of enterprise and workmen. So necessary did the inflow of capital seem to him for the success of a protectionist policy that, in his view, "duties ought only to be increased in the ratio in which capital, technical abilities and the spirit of enterprise are increasing in the nation or are being attracted to it from abroad". Finally, he would regard protection itself as the best instrumentality for securing the nationalisation of the foreign capital employed in the country.

Not less favourable were the views of another protectionist classic—Alexander Hamilton—to the admission of foreign

*List, *op. cit.*, pp. 183, 250-251 and 297.

capital: "It is not impossible" he observes "that there may be persons disposed to look with a jealous eye on the introduction of foreign capital as if it were an instrument to deprive our own citizens of the profits of our own industry. But perhaps there never could be a more unreasonable jealousy. Instead of being viewed as a rival, it ought to be considered as a most valuable auxiliary, conducing to put in motion a greater quantity of productive labour and a greater portion of useful enterprise than could exist without it. It is at least evident that in a country situated like the United States, with an infinite fund of resources yet to be unfolded, every farthing of foreign capital which is laid out in internal meliorations and in industrial establishments of a permanent nature is a precious acquisition."

The views of Carey and Roscher in favour of regarding the introduction of foreign capital and talents as indispensable to the success of protection have been thus summarised:—"One can say that the industrial transformation of the states entering economic civilization after others is due to foreign capital. On this matter, Carey and Roscher are in agreement." Indeed the same authority adds that, in effect, the orientation of national activities towards industry depends much more on the availability of capital than on the effects of protection as such.*

The pages of writers like Grunzel (who have made a special study of "commercial policy") might be ransacked in vain for reliable weapons of the protectionist armoury to be utilised against foreign capital or enterprise. Grunzel does not approve of foreign influence entering along the foreign capital, but he would not employ any means by which "the country would be deprived of that productive factor which in the course of modern development has become most important". He further admits that the various devices adopted by Germany to prevent the denationalisation of certain great enter-

*Fontana-Russo, *op. cit.*, p. 201.

prises like the Hamburg—America line proved to be failures. In view of the recommendation made by the Minority of the Indian Fiscal Commission that a certain proportion of directors should be citizens of the country, it might be noted that similar measures were adopted and proved useless in Germany. "It was along this line that were re-framed the statutory changes relating to this Hamburg—America Line in 1902. But even this device does not afford certain protection. When a majority of the shares are in the hands of foreigners it will not be difficult to find citizens for all the important positions, who will obediently follow the dictates of those whom they serve." In fact Grunzel is highly optimistic and argues that foreign enterprises always end in being absorbed by the country in which they are started and that it is unnecessary to adopt any special policy for nations with that object. "The purely private economic enterprises will succumb of themselves to the nationalisation process when the time comes. No encouragement in this direction through economic protective measures has proved itself desirable."*

Thus the great protectionist writers, with the lessons of a century of protectionism before them,. cannot suggest any means of keeping out foreign capital and enterprise, nor indeed do they think such an object a desirable one. On the other hand they speak in terms of approval of the encouragement afforded to the immigration of foreign business enterprise. Thus, Grunzel tells us how after the enactment of the customs tariff of 1906 was broughtabout in Austria, the central committee for the promotion of the industrial development of the Erzgebirg district addressed a circular letter to the German Chambers of Commerce setting forth that their region offered most favourable opportunities for the establishment of branch factories. Similarly he adds that in Russia the textile industry of Lodz owed its flourishing condition to Austrians and Germans who were no

*Grunzel, *op. cit.*, pp. 262-266; 330.

longer able to market their goods on account of increased duties. Thus, on the one hand the experience of foreign countries in the matter of restrictive measures adopted against foreign capital is not of an encouraging character, while on the other hand those countries which have admitted foreign capital and enterprise have benefited by such action.*

Employment of foreign capital, the condition of the success of Protection.

Apart from the importation of foreign capital, the next important financial resource of protectionism is perceived by the continental economists to be "the transformation of capital", *i.e.*, its transference from unprotected to protected industries. It being abundantly clear that protection cannot by itself add to the capital, the only alternatives are either to import capital or to transfer capital from old industries to the new and protected manufactures. There is always some friction and loss in this process of transference of capital. The danger is greatest when the protection is of a heavy and indiscriminating character. "That sort of protection will be always condemnable which, on account of its intense and irrational nature, causes a withdrawal of capital from its normal employments in order to transfer it to those employments which cannot give good results were they deprived of artificial support". On the other hand if protection withdraws capital from less remunerative industry to such industry as may after a short delay, and without artificial support yield higher profits, such a policy is praiseworthy.

We have already reviewed the possible directions from which capital resources could be possibly obtained in the case of India to assist a development of industries based on protection. We have seen that we cannot expect much from what is called the hoarded wealth; and that we could not and should not expect to divert agricultural capital and savings towards manu-

*Grunzel, *op. cit.*, pp. 271-272.

facture. In other countries the accumulations provided by older industries are vastly greater than in India; at present in our country except two or three mature industries all the others must be considered as infant industries. Consequently the relative demands of what must be considered as young industries bear a much larger proportion to our home resources of capital than is the case in other countries. Hence the supreme importance of the employment of foreign capital in the interest of the progress and development in India.

Conditions of exploitation by foreign capital.

The above reasoning does not preclude the possibility of the existence of conceivable cases where foreign enterprise in a country amounts to exploitation and where legislative powers have advisedly to be exercised to remedy matters. There is the case where foreign enterprise forms itself into a monopoly and is exploiting the consumer while closing opportunities of competition to its local rival. There is another situation of the same character where the great foreign firm starts branches and stifles local competition by unfair competitive devices. The condition precedent of the admission of foreign enterprise into India must be that they are purely competitive enterprises and that they maintain the proper plane of competition. This is an essential condition, because the burden of protection can only be decreased by the growth of *competing producers* within the country. Competitive conditions should be maintained at all costs, but so long as they are maintained there can be no question of exploitation by foreign capital.

In general however the fear of exploitation by foreign capital and enterprise is a reminiscence of bygone conditions when foreign enterprise enjoyed a monopolistic position and profits owing to the absence of any competetion from local enterprise or capital. To-day our capital is leaving off its negative attitude towards industries; we have produced entrepreneurs capable of handling very large industrial undertakings; and we enjoy access to the largest market for capital and to the best technical skill. Our altered political position has, if we make use of it in the right way, closed the gates of any adventitious assistance to foreign rivals.

Unlikelihood of any great rush of foreign capital to India.

There is no doubt that the inauguration of protection tempts foreign enterprise and capital into a country, but the strength of this tendency is liable to be exaggerated; and at the present time there are counteracting forces to be taken account of in a special degree. The Dominions Commission was dissatisfied with the rate at which British capital and enterprise was moving towards the Dominions in spite of the high protective tariffs. In the near future, on account of labour and other troubles and the rise of local costs of production the flow of foreign capital towards India is likely to be abnormally weak. The shortage of mobile capital throughout the world is another cause working in the same direction; and even when the general industrial depression wears off there will be accummulated calls on foreign capital in its own home. Foreign capital has not shown itself too ready of late to enter the Indian field even with the prospective co-operation of the leading industrial firms of our country and with the Indian tariff high enough to give a fair amount of incidental protection. In some cases in which the alliance of foreign capitalists was sought recently they, while agreeing to contribute their organizing power and capital, tried to shun the local risks and asked to be allotted a considerable proportion of safe debentures. The fact is, that here too the effects of tariff in causing movements of capital have been exaggerated and there are other forces much more powerful affecting its migration. The potential mobility of capital has no doubt been increasing, but at present and for much time to come, foreign capital is and will be both scarce and shy. We must not let ourselves argue from the unexpected ease with which our country has been securing government loans into the view that capital is eager to rush into India into industrial enterprises with all their risks and without any government guarantee. There are unmistakable signs that if industrial capital migrates to India it will be in alliance with well-established Indian firms, and even these latter have not been too successful of late in drawing capital from abroad.

The Indian as the natural heir of foreign enterprise.

It is often forgotten that the Indian is the natural heir of any foreign enterprise started in India. The foreign entrepreneur must sell out his securities when he retires to his country and by such transactions they ultimately pass into Indian hands. Even in the case of many Jute Mills of Bengal started by the "clannish" Scotchmen more than half of the shares have passed into Indian hands; and the process is still continuing. Foreign enterprise has given us a greater Dundee in Bengal, and we are now entering gradually on that inheritance; we ought to have done so long ago with a little more initiative. As it is, in many of the jute mills the Indians own the majority of shares and it is in their power to appoint Indian directors if they really desired that consummation. Talking of foreign enterprises, Grunzel observes, "The purely private economic enterprises will succumb of themselves to the naturalisation process when the time comes. No encouragement in this direction through economic protective measures has proved itself desirable."

Advantage of admitting foreign enterprise.

The beneficial effect of foreign capital and organizing power and technical skill cannot be too highly estimated. Until very lately Indan capital was prone to seek industries in which the certainty of success had been demonstrated; and though this state of things has altered for the better yet the industrial development of India implies the need of so much fresh capital and the inception of so many industries that the gain from foreign initiative will be incalculable. The industries to be developed are not only numerous and new but highly complicated in their technique, and gigantic in the matter of mass production and utilization of byproducts. Under such circumstances, one would agree with Mr. Manmohandas Ramji who expressed an opinion before the Indian Fiscal Commission in favour of "letting foreign entrepreneurs try the initial experiments for my country at his charge and expense." We cannot neglect the influence of the impetus and the momentum afforded by foreign capital and the working of foreign enterprise amongst us to the local capital and enterprise. Comparing the two great instrumentalities for affording a stimulus to local enterprise—viz. protectionist tariffs and example afforded by the working of the foreign capital and enterprise one would be inclined to give even more importance to the latter under proper circumstances. Foreign capital and enterprise working in our midst can alone give us the most important factor of success—the industrial environment and atmosphere.

It has often been urged that it is to our advantage to admit foreign capital but not the foreign entrepreneur, the objection to the latter course being that the profits made by him will leave the country. It is submitted here, however, that the problem is not so simple as to be decided in this way and that there are important considerations which deserve to be taken into account but which are often neglected in the ordinary reasoning on the subject. Let us compare the consequences of the two alternative courses—that of admitting foreign capital by itself and that of admitting the foreign entrepreneur with the capital.

The less expensive method.

In the case where foreign capital as well as organisation are allowed to enter the country the establishment of the industry taken in hand by them is rapid and certain. The foreign entrepreneur brings with him his whole experience and a fully developed industrial organisation as well as his capital. To admit him is to admit an industry in its entirety.

It is true that the country has to pay a price for the industry in as much as the profits go to the foreigner as long as his interest has not been bought up by the children of the soil.

But there is also a price to be paid by the country in the other case where only the foreign capital is imported and the task of developing an industry is left to local organisation. Here the cost of preliminary experiments is borne by the Indian entrepreneurs who have to buy their experience. The cost of industrial experiments on the modern manufacturing scale is enormous. So far again as foreign managers have to be hired to assist local entrepreneurs they have not only to be paid, but as experience in some directions has shown, they can create for themselves a position of power and patronage owing to the restricted knowledge and experience of their Indian employers. Owing to these unfavourable circumstances the *nascent stage of the industries is a prolonged one and the Indian consumer is mulcted for several decades in the shape of high prices.*

The fact is that in both cases the country has to pay a price for the establishment of the new industry. In one case the price consists of the profits which go to foreigner for a certain period—the length of the period depending upon the capital resource and the enterprise available in India for buying up the securities of the foreign establishment. In the other case where foreign capital alone is availed of by India the price is paid by the consumer for a very much longer time. It is for the country to judge in which of these two ways the price to be paid for industrial success is the smaller.

The practical difficulties in the way of any policy of restricting the entry of foreign capital and enterprise are very great.

Proposed restrictions on foreign industrial enterprise.

To illustrate this position we might examine some of the proposals on the subject which were placed before the Indian Fiscal Commission. It has been often urged that by law half the capital and management in all firms should be reserved for Indians. Such a scheme would restrict the full liberty of all parties to sell or purchase the shares of such concerns irrespective of colour or nationality. The scheme must also have a corollary by which Indian firms once floated should be prevented from allotting or allowing the transfer of more than 50 per cent. of their shares to Englishmen or foreigners. Such a proposal would not only create two markets for shares of the same firm but would also go against the principle of freedom of contract of which the transferability of shares is an important application.

We shall find other such proposals surrounded with similar difficulties. Let us take up first that one which would enforce mixed boards of directors. Under such a scheme, if the directorships are to be divided in proportion to the shares held by men of the two races, there must be a constant change in the racial proportions of the directors as the result of the sale and purchase of shares. On the other hand, if a fixed proportion of directors must be Indians irrespective of efficiency or of the holdings of the shares in Indian hands, the flow of foreign capital is sure to be greatly discouraged. Finally, let us look at another proposal which has been advanced under highly influential auspices and which is to the effect that the state in India should reserve the right of buying up all foreign concerns on terms and conditions that might be settled by the Government. Now, it is true that a similar policy was followed successfully with reference to Indian railways; but then these latter enterprises had been assisted by the state at their inception, and had further been allotted a term of years before which they could not be bought out. It is also difficult to see on what fair basis the Government could fix the price of these concerns. Would the country gain much or anything if the price paid was based, as it should be on present as well as prospective profits? And to whom and on what principle is the state to transfer the businesses thus acquired? Above all, it is hardly to be expected that foreign industrialists would take the risks of starting concerns which could be bought up by the Government if and as soon as they proved successful.

The Minority of the Indian Fiscal Commission proposed that all foreign companies should in future be incorporated and registered in India in Rupee Capital. One can sympathise with the idea underlying the proposal. But as a matter of fact, the recommendation if carried out will result in a somewhat superfluous measure since there are very strong economic forces working in the direction already, with the result that the proportion of companies incorporated elsewhere and working in India is comparatively speaking very small indeed. Moreover, it is easy to exaggerate the beneficial results of such a proposal as has been pointed out. This measure as well as the other restrictions proposed by the minority can do little to prevent the profits of the foreign enterprises leaving the country. It needs to be noted that the Company Legislation of the world might be searched in vain for any parallel to many of the proposals which have been put forward on the subject.

Views of leading industrialists of India.

The views of the ablest Indian publicists and captains of industry can be shown to be favourable to the unrestricted inflow of foreign capital and enterprise. The late Sir V. Thackersey in his evidence before the Indian Fiscal Commission declared that he would welcome the advent of foreign firms in India except where they tried to secure special concessions. So also Mr. Manmohandas Ramji in his evidence expressed the view that foreign capital and enterprise if allowed to enter India freely would give at their own cost practical experience of industrial matters to the Indians. He went on to say that if restrictive conditions were prescribed for the employment of such capital, and the foreign entrepreneurs were consequently prevented from investing their capital in India, it would be stopping the prosecution of very important industries in the country merely on sentimental grounds. Consequently, Mr. Ramji declared himself against the proposal to insist on a certain percentage of capital and managing appointments being reserved for Indians in any enterprises. Even so far as concessions are concerned, provided equal opportunities were afforded to Indians and Englishmen he would place no barrier against the latter.

The views and the practice of the Tatas as regards the utilization of foreign capital and organizing power are well-known. Another great Indian captain of industry—Sir R. Mookerjee—has strongly recommended the free admission of foreign capital into India. His views were fully expressed before the Indian Industrial Conference of 1911. "We often see articles in Indian newspapers, or hear speeches from public platforms condemning the use of foreign (English) capital for the development of Indian industries. But I am afraid, those who hold such views do not seriously consider the question in all its aspects. Apart from the fact that foreign capital is only attracted by signs of peace and prosperity, and that we know that foreign capital is welcome in any other country for the development of her industries, an important consideration for us in India arises from the fact that, for our own good, it is wise to allow British capitalists to interest themselves in our industries, and thus take an active part in their development." In a similar view the Hon'ble Mr. Harkishenlal emphasised the necessity of "coaxing" foreign capital into India before the Indian Industrial Conference of 1912.

Before the Indian Fiscal Commission similar views were expressed by Mr. B. F. Madon, a well-known Indian writer on economic topics. If the foreign firms come here with their own capital and take their own risks, he said, "I do not want to have any proportion of Indians in them. That would not be fair." As to the proposed restrictions, he added, "I personally don't see any good in it, because we are in such a backward state that it would be in the interests of the country even to have industries started by foreigners. So far as the foreign firms come in at their own risk they were to be welcomed since they would bring with them their own processes, methods and organization: While they got the benefit of the tariff the country would benefit in its turn by the introduction of new methods and the training of Indian labour." Where, however, such companies claimed Government patronage, Mr. Madon would have the Government see that they were Indian not merely in name but in fact.

The above views of our leading organizers of industry are powerfully reinforced by the reasoning and eloquence of a great publicist like Sir P. S. Sivaswamy Iyer. In a recent speech he observed: "English capital, English business knowledge and English technical skill ought to be specially welcome in this connection (Indian mercantile marine). It is one of the unfortunate results of the movement that is now stirring the country that there is a deplorable feeling of an anti-English character which may dispose people to reject aid from English sources. But if we remember that our own capital is utterly inadequate for all the purposes of development of the country, if we remember that the Britisher is supreme in many spheres and specially in the sphere of ship-building, of maritime enterprise and of banking, it would be foolish on our part not to invite the co-operation and the aid of English business knowledge and English capital. *I will therefore welcome the co-operation of the Briton in advancing this object as well as many other objects which are dear to us all, for the purpose of promoting the development of the country.*"

Our conclusion is that there are strong reasons for pausing before adopting any course which restricts the free flow of foreign capital into India. We have to consider the fact that conditions essential to exploitation by foreign capital are a matter of the past, so far as India is concerned; that a vast amount of foreign capital is essential for anything like an adequate industrial development of the country; that under present circumstances of the world's capital resources, nothing like this adequate supply of foreign capital is likely to be attracted to the country; that artificial remedies for the nationalisation of foreign capital have not proved successful in any country; finally, that the competition of foreign capital would lighten the burden of protection on the Indian consumer, would shorten the period of infancy of our industries and would give us the much needed experience, organisation and industrial environment. Nothing is to be lost by delaying the formulation of a policy of a restrictive character until we can read the signs of the times. If it should appear that under protection a plethora of foreign capital is being attracted towards India, then it will be time enough for us to impose what conditions we choose, and the foreign capitalist will comply with them in his own interests. If, however, as is for more likely to be the case, there is no considerable rush of capital in our direction, we need be in no hurry to block up the slender stream by the adoption of artificial restrictions.

LECTURE VII.

IMPERIAL PREFERENCE.

The labours of the Indian Fiscal Commission in the matter of Imperial Preference have resulted in the formulation of such a narrower range and scope of that policy as is adapted to the circumstances of India, as well as in the provision of suitable and efficient safeguards of the interests of the Indian producer and consumer. But the proposals of the Commission were based upon the long and instructive discussions of the earlier and far more extensive proposals for Imperial Preference. These discussions have thrown light on all the potentialities of Imperial Preference, and they comprise not only the work of two committees but quite a number of controversial writings. It is necessary to refer briefly to these earlier discussions in order to explain the position taken up by the Commission and the significance of the proposals emanating from it.

The opinions of Lord Curzon's Government in India were generally unfavourable to the inauguration of the policy of Preference by India. No other result could indeed have been expected since, as the Government of India's letter observes, "the recommendation in favour of preferential tariffs was of an extremely general and indefinite character. . . . There is nothing before us in the nature of a definite scheme on the suitability of which to Indian circumstances we can pronounce with confidence". As has been emphasised later by Lord Ronaldshay,* there is nothing in the memorandum in question to support the contention that the Government of India would have been unwilling to discuss proposals for reciprocal trade concessions. Some years later, Sir Edward Law one of the signatories of

*Earl of Ronaldshay, *An Eastern Miscelleny*, Chapter 13 & 14.

the Despatch of 1903 declared that it was for the Home Government "to formulate such proposals as will justify India in accepting the policy of Imperial Preference and such proposals can be formulated." But the question was in fact presented to the Indian Government of the day in the most dogmatic and in the least attractive shape. In giving an adverse opinion, it specified three consideratons which led it to that view—the potential difficulties regards India's finances, the absence of any great advantage either to Great Britain or to India, and finally, the fear of retaliation. Further, under the then existing circumstances, the Government were led to assume the incompatibility of a policy of Imperial Preference with that of protection for Indian industries ; and while they showed by their remarks that they would welcome the existence of tariff conditions which would enable them to retaliate on or negotiate with other countries they could not anticipate that two decades later India would have a decisive voice as regards both Preference and a protectionist tariff. In fact a great many important considerations detract from the utility of the Memorandum of 1903 for the present controversy—the then absence of anything like fiscal auonomy for India, the consequent impossibility of anything like a protectionist tariff, the predominance of British manufactures in the Indian market, and the fact that the issue of Preference was in those days presented to India in its most vague, dogmatic and uninviting shape and form.

The Memorandum considered the financial effects of the policy of Imperial Preference in its two main aspects. In the first place, it was assumed in the absence of fiscal autonomy that the method by which preference would be accorded would be by a reduction of the duties on British goods. It could not be foreseen at the time that some years later India would be in the same—or nearly the same—position as the Dominions in the matter of a *pari passu* prosecution of the policies of Preference and protection. Consequently, it was inferred that a certain result of the introduction of Preference would be the loss of customs revenue. Such conclusions were in those days unavoidable in the absence of the power to overhaul and readjust the whole range of customs duties to the advantage of the Indian treasury. The memorandum, however, added another financial consideration which should still be regarded as a very strong, if not, indeed, a decisive argument against any *general* scheme of Imperial Preference. India, it was argued, is a debtor country with the obligation of paying several millions per annum in a currency different from that in which her own revenues are collected. Hence the imperative necessity, as far as she is concerned, of preserving an equivalent excess of exports over imports. It is therefore, a vital object with her to stimulate her exports by every means in her power. Should Imperial Preference lead to tariff wars, such an excess of export, which India possesses normally would be destroyed. She would, as a consequence be not only unable to meet her obligations, but her currency system would also receive a rude shock. The Government of India might have easily strengthened its case at this particular point by statistical considerations. It has been often noted, that while our trade with the British Empire has generally given us an adverse balance, our trade with foreign countries presents the opposite aspect. As a young and gifted Indian economist has stated "if the full programme of Imperial Preference were adopted, with preferential import as well as export duties, while imports from the British Empire would increase, exports to foreign countries would decline, and the balance of trade would turn against us." This is the strongest argument, as has been said, against a general and comprehensive scheme of Preference.

The argument urged against Imperial Preference on the ground of potential retaliation is not nearly so strong, and, as will be seen its force has been steadily declining in the decades which have elapsed since the Memorandum was drafted, with the vast growth of Preferential policies in other Empires. What was then regarded as a novelty has now become a common fiscal policy of all great political units. Even in 1903, Sir Edward Law was confident as regards India's position in the case of attempted reprisals. "I feel sufficiently confident that with the great majority of the countries with which we trade, and as regards the very great bulk of our exports of raw material, we are not only in a safe position, but we could even afford, in certain cases, ourselves to assume the aggressive by going so far as to impose duties on the exportation of produce they require for their industries". Such was his confident view as regards the possiblities of retaliation. That it was not merely a theoretical position was shown by the experiment in countervailing duties against bounty-fed sugar which had been carried out at the time. Nor did the fear of reprisals prevent the Indian Government of the day from desiring to launch out into a policy of retaliation. It is curious to hear it express its fear of reprisals and its belief in its powers of efficacious retaliation in the same breath. There could be no country against which some measure of retaliation is not possible; but, comparatively speaking, few countries can be said to be so secure in the matter. This is shown clearly by fact that while the policy of protection is on the *tapis,* no apprehensions have been expressed as regards the dangers of retaliation, in any quarter. In fact the argument from retaliation is the weakest that could be directed against the adoption of Imperial Preference by India.

The statement of the Hon'ble Sir C. Innes at the Economic Conference of 1923 forms a supplement to Lord Curzon's Despatch of 1903. The dicta of the Hon'ble Mr. Innes are valid as regards their condemnation of a *general* scheme of Imperial Preference and it is easy to agree with him "that it would be difficult for India in the present circumstances to embark on a general policy of Imperial Preference and to set up what may be called a 'two-decker' tariff." While condemning unreservedly such a general scheme of Preference, Mr. Innes asserted the potentialities latent in the policy of judiciously limited Preference as advocated by the Indian Fiscal Commission. He observed that he might "reasonably be asked whether even granting that a general preferential tariff is at present out of question, some measure of preference could not be given, at any rate in respect of some of the items in our tariff schedule, especially as valuable tariff concessions have been made to India, not only by His Majesty's Government, but also by New Zealand and Canada." On this point, after acknowledging that the concessions received by India are particularly valuable in respect of tea, tobacco and coffee, he observed: "The course I have mentioned would not be open, at any rate in the same degree, to the economic objections I have taken to a general preferential tariff, and it is perhaps a possible line of advance." Further, as the question of preference based on reciprocity was not referred to him he naturally made no observations on that proposal for which there is even a stronger case than for preference on a limited and restricted scale.

A new conception of the scope of preference.

The topic of Imperial Preference had so far called forth a considerable literature besides two public inquiries. The Fiscal Commission had enjoyed the benefit of these studies and its recommendations are based on them. These recommendations consist of the *formulations of a series of limitations* within which preference might be granted with the approval of the Indian Legislature. The limitations are calculated to emphasise the new *enunciation of Imperial Preference* as a policy which could be voluntarily and reasonably adopted consistently with our interests to promote inter-imperial trade and the manufactures of the mother country. The idea of any joint-tariff policy of the Empire imposed on the component parts is expressly disavowed. The limitations are so formulated as to make the criticisms which used to be justifiably advanced against the larger and, it might be added—cruder—schemes of preference applicable no longer.

The first limitation consists of the assertion that any general system of preference is out of question and that any preference granted should be in consequence of a sporadic of a or rather *selective and discriminating character.* This proposal was a logical one, on the part of a commission which has decided for discriminating protection as against a general protection. If protection is to be given after an inquiry into the concrete facts of each industry, so must be Preference. This is further emphasised by the principle laid down that such Preference as is given should not impose an appreciable burden on the Indian consumer. It used to be argued, with a good deal of justification, that any general scheme of Preference would unfavourably affect the balance trade of India, since its exports to foreign countries are of much greater value than its imports from those countries. But, from the present scheme of preference, applied to a few and well-chosen articles, no such results need be feared. The United Kingdom has herself set us the example in 1919, by initiating a scheme of Preference including a limited range of articles such as suited herself. That scheme is a very different one from, and on a much more modest scale than, the vast and ambitious scheme of Chamberlain. Indeed, there is a general tendency to restrict and to define more closely the scope of a policy of preference.

The second limitation suggested by the Fiscal Commission is that no Preference should be given in such a way as to diminish the protection required by and afforded to Indian industries. The example of the Dominions has shown that Imperial

Compatibility of Protection of Preference.

Preference is perfectly compatible with protection to domestic industires, even when the former is adopted on a much more liberal scale than has been contemplated by the Indian Fiscal Commission. In numerous instances the Dominions increased duties on British imports, on the ground that local industries must receive the first consideration, and that only after they are duly protected should preference be given to British against foreign trade. To take one example—Canada has proceeded tentatively in this matter raising preferential duties in some directions whenever local manufacturers have complained and lowering them in other directions whenever experience had shown the possibility. In India we have the Tariff Board which can study and advise upon the proper relations to be adopted between preference and protection so as to prevent any encroachments on the latter.

How the interest of the consumer is to be guarded.

It is obvious that any scheme of general or indiscriminate Preference is ruled out by a due regard to the interests of the Indian consumer and producer. In order to minimise the burden to the consumer, Preference should be extended only as regards those commodities for the production of which Great Britian possesses potential capacities virtually as good as those possessed by its foreign rivals. To put it in technical language, the elasticity of supply of the particular industry in Great Britain should be likely ultimately to equal or even to exceed that of the same industry situated in foreign countries. Should preference be given to commodities selected on this principle the burden to the Indian consumers would be small or even nil. On this point the views of a wellknown authority on problems of international trade might be inserted with advantage:—"If the favoured country can increase its production so as to progress with or even beyond the increase of demand, *i.e.*, if competition in that country establishes the same conditions as if its rivals had not been excluded, then not only would these latter have to abandon all hopes of sharing the preferential market, but the favoured producers will bear part or even the whole of the preferential duty. It is certain that in such circumstances the local consumers would receive the same advantages as if no restraints had been placed on the foreign competition. We can say that the preference might secure positive advantage to the local consumer if under its stimulus the producers in the favoured region will augment their production so as to exceed the total former supply." It must be admitted, that we can only rarely come across a concurrence of circumstances so eminently favourable to the adoption of Preference. The contention advanced here is, however, that Preference should not be extended to articles regarding which the elasticity of the foreign supply is markedly greater than that of the corresponding British supply.*

There prevailed a fear in many quarters that the interests of India would not be considered of paramount importance in fixing a policy of preference. It has been observed recently that fiscal autonomy for India does not rest on a statutory basis but only on a convention. But precedents show that fiscal autonomy has always grown from more to more by the road of convention. This convention is reinforced by the express recommendations of the Indian Fiscal Commission that no preference should be granted on any articles without the explicit approval of the Indian Legislature. In this way an extension of Fiscal autonomy is made a condition precedent to the inauguration of Preference, and later events might easily show that there is a great deal of interaction between the rise and progress of fiscal autonomy and imperial preference. It needs no great prophetic power to trace some measure of correlation between Imperial Preference and fiscal autonomy—between the assumption by India of some at least of the sacrifices of imperial responsibility and the recognition of India as an equal partner of the Empire.

It might be asked what value is to be attached to preference

*Fontana-Russo, *op. cit.*, pp. 591-592.

thus limited and defined and which would not involve any tangible economic loss to India? The question deserves to be answered and the objection to be met. England is a country which supplies a large proportion of the manufactures consumed in neutral markets, and any tangible preference shown to its wares in particular directions in these days of very keen competition would have a beneficial influence. In the long period of commercial and industrial depression which seems to await the world, even small advantages are not without their value. There is also the moral influence and stimulus of regarding India as a market favourably inclined towards British competition as against foreign manufacturers. In the case of some articles the English producer might be just being supplanted by the foreign and here a little preference might not be without its value. Some of these "selected cases" are enumerated in the Fiscal Commission Report and others might be found out by the Tariff Board. Lastly, there are to be considered a few cases where the Indian producer might need more protection against the foreign producer than against the Britisher. It has also to be remembered that the scheme of preference might be supplemented by reciprocity agreements concluded on equal terms by India, which might bring mutual advantages.

Comparing the potential gains of India and of the Dominions from an adoption of Imperial Preference we find the advantage resting with the former. A high American authority* has pointed out that such preferences as England has given under the programme of 1919 are of interest chiefly to India and the Colonies, and because of the limited range of articles covered by that preference scheme, there is little in them of value to the self-governing dominions. The preference given on tea—two pence a pound—is of importance to us owing to the growing and severe competition of the tea from Sumatra and Java. There are two other preferences—on coffee and tobacco—which

**Colonial Tariff Policies.* (Washington) 1922.

might be of interest to India if properly manipulated. Under the scheme for preference as laid down by the Commission, India will be making a much smaller sacrifice than the Dominions and will secure a larger share of such gain as the preference can yield. If we look at the list of articles on which the United Kingdom gives preferences we find in it several staple exports of India, Mauritius and British West Indies, but none of Canada, Australia or South Africa. But, there is a wider point of view from which the potential gains of India might be contemplated. It is well-known that many articles as regards which India's position as exporter was once unrivalled are now being largely produced elsewhere and hence there is the prospect of constantly keener competition with Indian exports. Thus, Argentina is increasing her competition with India as regards oil seeds. Java is a most formidable rival as regards tea. As regards rice the competition from French Colonies in the Far East is steadily increasing. In our exports of groundnuts we are experiencing heavier competition. Indeed, it is very probable that some European powers will develop their African Colonies in such a way that the predominance of India as an exporter of raw materials might be challenged further and in other directions. It is, of course true, that countries exporting raw materials have the whip-hand of those dependent upon their exports of manufactures. At the same time the development of new colonies and protectorates is a source of constantly growing competition for the lands exporting raw materials predominantly. Hence, the growing importance of Imperial preference where it is practicable.

Fears of retaliation.

The fear of Retaliation following on the introduction of preference has been greatly reduced by the march of events, especially when preference is granted on a moderate scale. But there is another factor which has been tending steadily to reduce the possibilities of retaliation since the days of Lord Curzon's inquiry. Policies of "assimilation" or preference have been adopted by all great commercial countries—by the U.S.A., France, Holland, Italy and Japan. What all practice no one can condemn or treat as a cause of provocation and retaliation. Thus France has adopted "tariff—assimilation" "as its prevailing policy" as regards its largest colonies Algeria, Indo-China, Tunis, Madagascar, etc. With regard to the other French colonies also there are preferential arrangements. Italian Colonies also grant large preferences to national goods. Since 1909, Japan applied the policy of tariff-assimilation to Formosa, Saghalien, etc., &c. ; since 1920 the same policy has been applied to Korea. The United States, too, pursue the policy of preferential trade relations with its colonies. In fact there is no power with anything like over-seas Dominions, which has not developed preferential duties. What all therefore practise no one can make a ground of retaliation.

Since the Fiscal Commission expressed itself in favour of a discriminating or selective system of Imperial Preference it is a well to indicate how such a system of differential import duties could be employed so as to entail the minimum of sacrifice or burden whether for the Indian consumer or producer. As regards the producer's interests they would be safeguarded in any event if such legitimate protection as he is entitled to is preserved intact. With regard to the Indian consumer the problem is more complicated and we mrst borrow some light from the general theory of the incidence of differential duties. The chief rule which we ought the conform is, that in the interest of the consumer we should advisedly place the smaller import duty on the produce from the more "elastic" (or expansible) source of supply ; otherwise, we practically compel our consumer to have resort to the less efficient source of supply. That source possesses *ex-hypothesi* fewer economies and potentialities of production, and consequently it has the larger costs of production at present or in future. To take an illustration, if I may buy an article from two rival factories, it would pay me to encourage by my custom that one of the two establishments which possesses favourable potentialities for manufacturing more and cheaper the article which I purchase. To take another example, *if* the facilities possessed by Lancashire for furnishing increased supplies of cotton goods of the sort required by the Indian were greater than those possessed by other countries, there would be justification for levying the smaller import duty on the goods coming from Lancashire.

The above principle and its corollaries constitute the theoretical basis of a judicious application of Imperial Preference. Generally speaking, provided the inter-imperial sources are found to be able to supply the whole volume of goods of a particular kind required by us, as well as the foreign sources, a preferential import duty would hardly entail a sacrifice on the Indian consumer, because under such circumstances we could count on competition for our custom within the empire to reduce the sacrifice to our consumer. To take a concrete example of this case, if an English-made article was losing ground in our markets only through unfair competition or through circumstances of a temporary character, we can well afford to extend our assistance to it. In the second place, even if the British sources of production could not supply the whole of the Indian requirements for the article in question at once, it might be conceivable that some preference shown by India might lead to the expansion of the industry which could ultimately supply the article as cheaply as the foreign source. In fact, there is a close parallel between Imperial Preference and protection and the considerations favouring each of them. In either case the domestic consumer might suffer to some extent at the start by the restriction of his sources of supply. In both cases we can count upon the growth of the scale of the industries concerned and of internal competition to lower the prices ultimately. On the same ground neither protection nor preference could be recommended if the source of supply which is proposed to be assisted suffers from a comparative inelasticity of supply.

So far we have considered the lines on which and the extent to which India should grant preference to Great Britain without raising the question of any *quid pro quo*. But it appears highly probable that in time to come the scope of preference will be largely expanded on the basis of reciprocity agreements. Even at present a great deal of inter-colonial trade is regulated by such agreements. Thus Canada extended preference to South Africa (1904) and to British West Indies (1920-21) by special argeements. Similarly Australia extended protection to South Africa (1906) only after negotiation and agreements. It certainly appears more patriotic to make free gifts to the Mother country; but it prevents the economic solidarity of the Empire from being broadbased on a system of treaties. There is great room to supplement the free-will offerings which the Indian Fiscal Commission has recommended by businesslike compacts on much wider lines. We must certainly begin with the free-concessions recommended by the Commission; but such a system of free concessions between England and India corresponds only to the exchange of ceremonial "nuzranas" or complimentary gifts, exchanged between exalted personages; no extensive business dealings can be transacted on such a ceremonial basis. Free-will concessions will always be on a somewhat limited scale; but the scope of commercial agreements can be—and indeed will be—automatically extended as economic development goes on throughout the entire Empire, and the need is felt for asking favourable treatment in new directions.

A plea for Imperial Reciprocity.

We have seen that the first advocates of Imperial Preference in India proposed the establishment of a comprehensive and general system of preferential rates. The Indian Fiscal Commission has seen the inadvisability of such a comprehensive system and prefers to restrict the scope of Imperial Preference to a group of selected articles on which preference should be given. We have seen further that if preference is to obtain an extended scope as desired it should realise in itself *the idea of Imperial reciprocity.* Indeed by that name, the movement which is generally called that of Imperial Preference, was actually designated by sponsors like Sir Vincent Caillard. It is only such an imperial reciprocity which " would stimulate and facilitate mutual commercial intercourse, and would by promoting the development of the resources and industries of the several parts, strengthen the Empire." There were quite a number of proponents of the idea of *reciprocal preference* at the Ottawa Colonial Conference of 1894 where the policy of preference was first broached.

Three phases of the idea of Preference.

Looking at the history of the movement towards Imperial Preference, we find that during the last thirty years there have been three distinct phases of the idea.

The *first phase* is naturally identified with the activity of Joseph Chamberlain in the cause. According to him Imperial Preference was to be initiated as a comprehensive and extensive system of rates, and to be born like Minerva in full panoply. Nor was this enough ; beyond it lay the prospect of Free-Trade within the Empire, and an advance towards this ideal was to be achieved by successive steps of preferential treatment. The scope of preference was taken to be the widest possible. Tariff walls were not to be raised by the colonies against British products, and where they existed they were to be generally lowered. Again, the colonies were to agree " not to enter upon the production of articles whose manufacture was not yet developed in the colonies but was important in the mother country." There was no question of individual bargaining between the recipients of preferential favours. Such thorough-going advocacy of Imperial Preference and such a wide conception of its scope did not fail in the end to injure the cause.

In the face of these difficulties, the advocates of preference began to reduce the scope of their policy, and there arose a tendency to restrict the application of such a policy to a limited range of articles. This might be called the *second phase* in the history of Imperial Preference. The best example of this tendency is to be found in the English Tariff Act of 1919. The scheme covers a strictly limited range of articles and the preferential rates are extended only to—tea, cocoa, coffee, chicory, currants, dried or preserved fruit, sugar, glucose, molasses, saccharin, motor-spirit, tobacco, wine and spirits. It was obviously felt that this was a comparatively small list of articles and one moreover, of little value at least to the self-governing Dominions. It was therefore added that this scheme did not comprise the whole of the Governments' preference policy. Preference "was to inform the whole of our policy"—in particular such capital issues which were to be expended in the Dominions were to be given preference. Little or nothing came, however, of this supplementary programme of preference.

In the colonies too, during this phase there was seen a restriction of the scope of preference. Thus in Canada the establishment of the Intermediate Tariff virtually circumscribed the amount of the British Preference after 1906; while the preference was further impaired by concessions to other countries. But for the defeat of the movement towards reciprocity with the United States of America the process of impairment would have gone on further. Australia too has introduced the principle of the intermediate tariff which cannot fail to reduce the scope of preference. In New Zealand the list of articles on which preference is given has been reduced and the preference has been affected by the desire to increase trade with America. In the case of all Dominions the reduction of Preference would have been much greater but for the patriotic fervour engendered by the great war.

The *third phase* of the idea of Imperial Preference has

come to the fore during the last few years. As we have seen, even at the Ottawa Colonial Conference of 1894 there were not a few partisans of *reciprocal preference* who raised the question of imperial reciprocity directly. But it required the long experience of preference to make it evident that if preference was to become a permanent as well as comprehensive policy it could only be on the basis of mutuality. This attitude has been emphatically expressed a couple of years ago by the Australian Minister for trade and customs. "While we are quite willing to accord this large measure of protection to British industry and give assistance to our kinsmen overseas", he stated, "I believe that *that policy cannot go on for ever without reciprocity.* I am very pleased to note that recently the British Parliament have made a start in the way of reciprocal relations with the Dominions. I hope it is only a beginning, and that the statesmen of Britain will see their way clear to recognize in some more substantial way than they have up to the present, the value of reciprocal trade relationship which we are endeavouring to strengthen in the proposals now before us. I admit there are peculiar difficulties surrounding the position of Great Britain; but, still, a start has been made, which I hope is the beginning of better things. As I say, while the commonwealth Government do not ask for a *quid pro quo, the present position, as I have said, cannot exist for all time.*"

In last year's Imperial Conference, the reciprocal character of Imperial Preference had been strongly emphasised. Sir Philip Lloyd Graeme had announced further specific proposals on behalf of the United Kingdom. Empire grown dried figs, raisins, plums and currants were to be admitted duty free. A new duty of 10*s*. 6*d*. per cwt. was to be imposed on foreign dried fruits like apples, pears and peaches, and a duty of 5*s*. on foreign preserved fruits. The then existing preference on sugar and tobacco was stabilised for ten years. These concessions on the part of the United Kingdom were of course expected to bring forward a response on the part of the Dominions. The idea of reciprocity as the basis of Preference was constantly brought forward at the Conference, and the Under Secretary for the Colonies made an appeal for reciprocity between the Crown Colonies and the Dominions. In the subsequent controversy the same idea has been kept to the fore. Thus the Canadian correspondent of the "Times" was of opinion that " if, as Mr. Asquith suggests, certain Dominion preferences were withdrawn it is almost certain that Canadian preferences in favour of British goods would be reduced. It is repeated on the other hand that, if a general preference policy were accepted by the Mother Country and developed to include food products, it is impossible to doubt that Canadian duties would be further lowered in favour of British manufacturers." We have obviously travelled very far since the days when it was said that the main thought of the advocates of preference was "moral and sympathetic unity", and that Colonial Preference was granted "not for the gain of the gold, the getting, the hoarding, the having". Mr. Bruce, the Australian Premier, in a speech at Lincoln emphasised the idea of reciprocity in Imperial Preference in a particularly aggressive style. Australia, according to him, was not there as a suppliant for trade relations in order to benefit herself to the detriment of Britain. She had already been approached by other countries for reciprocal treatment, but hitherto had refused offers because they would be detrimental to Great Britain.

There are ample indications in the evidence given before the Indian Fiscal Commission and in the report of that body that a system of preference based on reciprocity would be welcomed by many in this country. Thus the Hon'ble Mr. Harkishenlal argued before the Commission that "if the status of India is equal to (that of) other partners in the Empire, India should be prepared to adopt a preferential tariff in favour of other members against foreign countries *in return for equal economic advantages.* No appreciable economic loss to one country against another in the Empire is contemplated by economic equality." In his examination he agreed with Sir E. Holberton in defining Imperial Preference as "Empire trade treaties on mutually favourable terms." He added that the other meaning of the term was given to it by "a political rather than an economic man, Joseph Chamberlain, and he had a political game to play." In the opinion of the well-known financier and politician of the Punjab "India should be prepared to adopt it (Imperial Preference) if you could get rid of the idea that preference means loss to any body, and keep the idea that it means mutual relations, *i.e.*, reciprocity." In fact he made the acceptance of Imperial Preference by India depend upon two conditions—the contractual status of India should be equal to that of other partners of the Empire, and there should be an exchange of equal advantages. "Having these two conditions, I do not mind giving preferential treatment to other members of the Empire against foreign countries."

Nor is Mr. Harkishenlal's the only authoritative opinion advanced in India in favour of Imperial reciprocity. Mr. Sastri was reported to have expressed the view that he would not object to India being a party to a reciprocity agreement with Great Britain. But, as the Fiscal Commission had not the benefit of examining Mr. Sastri it had no opportunity of studying his views in detail. It was otherwise with the late Sir Vithaldas Thackersey. In his examination he laid down the principle that under what he called Imperial Preference "trade relations should be mutual and on a reciprocally advantageous footing". He wanted the Indian Legislature to decide whether in giving and taking preference "there was mutual and reciprocal advantage to both contracting parties." He went on to add the following dictum: "I am convinced that if we have a controlling voice and if we have reciprocal advantage then a policy of Imperial Preference would be advantageous both to us and to the Empire. But in the absence of such full control it may be dangerous."

The Hon'ble Mr. Kale, now a member of the Tariff Board, has also argued in his work on "Indian Economics" that when India has secured fiscal autonomy and equality of status with the Dominions, she should participate in Imperial Preference. "When these conditions are satisfied, it will be perfectly fair to expect from India all the sacrifices which Imperial responsibility will throw on her shoulders. The main object of Imperial Preference is the consolidation of the Empire and the promotion of its material prosperity . . . Imperial consolidation to be attained by preferential trade within the Empire, will, of course, entail *reciprocal* sacrifices, and the scheme must be such that each constituent part of the Empire will be called upon to make a reasonable contribution."

The above extracts must have shown the prevalence of the feeling that Imperial Preference must be of a reciprocal character in order to be generally acceptable. It is also easily shown that by far the greater part of inter-colonial preferences in the British Empire are based upon special agreements. This has been well brought about in a recent publication of the United States Tariff Commission. With certain exceptions, the inter-colonial trade of the British Empire does not rest upon the basis of the preferences granted to the mother country, except in so far as special agreements have been concluded. The dates in the following summary quoted from that publication are those of the introduction and chief revisions of the preferential rates; the preferences which have been extended only after negotiations and agreements are indicated by "Agr."

Tabular View of British Empire Preferences.

Preferences granted	To United Kingdom	To Canada	To New-Zealand	To Australia	To South Africa	To British West Indies	To some or all other Crown Colonies
By Canada	1898 1900 1904 1915		1904		1904 Agr.	1898 1912-13 Agr. 1920-21 Agr.	1898 1907 1913
By New Zealand	1903 1907 1917	The whole	Empire				
By South Africa	1903 1906 1915	1904 A r.	1906-07 Agr.	1906 Agr.			
By Australia	1907 1908 1911 1914 1920				1906 Agr.		
By British West Indies	1913 1920-21	1912-13 Agr. 1920-21 Agr.					
By United Kingdom By Cyprus By Fiji	1919 1920 1922	The whole	Empire				

Our conclusion is that the scheme of preference laid down by the Indian Fiscal Commission should, and will probably be extended largely by reciprocity agreements between all members of the Empire concluded on equal footing and terms. In the meanwhile and as a beginning, the scheme of preference in the Report has many advantageous features to recommend it. It deprives Preference of its former character of a general formula applicable automatically to a great range of articles; it limits our free-will concessions and offerings to a modest scale such as is commensurate with the limited capacity of our country to make any sacrifices of that kind, and compatible with the general expansion of the trade of India in all directions. The amount and scope of the preference should be such as should harmonise with our protectionist policy. The Indian Fiscal Commission has emphasised protection rather than preference and has followed the example of the Dominions therein. To refuse all Preference would be to decline to enter the commercial comity of the Empire as well as to ignore such benefits as India is already receiving from preferential treatment; while in granting Pre-ference on the lines recommended, we make a smaller sacrifice than the Dominions at the same time that we secure advantages larger than theirs.